LAX

OUT THE WINDOW (LAX)

02 [los angeles forum for architecture and urban design]

Published by
Los Angeles Forum for Architecture and Urban Design
PO Box 291774, Los Angeles CA 90029-8774

Texts by Pico Iyer, Norman M. Klein & Julian Myers

Published in the United States of America
ISBN 0-9763166-2-5

Cataloging-in-Publication data for this book is available from the Library of Congress

For Los Angeles Forum for Architecture and Urban Design

Printed and bound in China

LAX

OUT THE WINDOW (LAX)
photos by Zoe Crosher

WEST OF LA CIENEGA

LAX Radisson
LAX Courtyard by Marriott
LAX Sheraton Gateway
LAX Crowne Plaza
LAX Embassy Suites
LAX Four Points
LAX Renaissance
LAX Marriott
LAX Hilton
LAX Travelodge
LAX Westin
LAX Quality Inn (now the Clarion Hotel)
LAX Holiday Inn
LAX Hampton Inn

By Pico Iyer

THE SPACE BETWEEN ALL SPACES

In 1994 I went to live in Los Angeles Airport for a couple of weeks, taking it to be an emblem (though hardly an inspiring one) of the city of the future. All the cultures of the world assembled under a single roof, yet few of them sharing a common language. Passionate, life-changing moments – children taking off for war, parents met again after half a century, honeymooners and refugees and missionaries assembling – all set in a near-anonymous matrix of TCBY yogurt shops, Starbucks cafes and stores whose very names (The Nature Company) enforce a kind of placelessness. More than 23,000 parking spaces crowded in to accommodate a daily employee population twice the size of the entire principality of Monaco.

I wrote a long account of this unsettling, postmodern metropolis in my book *The Global*

Soul – LAX represents the spiritual home of a new, placeless, roaming and often dislocated population of sleepwalkers and speed-fliers – but getting it all down did not get LAX out of my system. Over and over, visiting my sometime home in Santa Barbara, I found myself revisiting its spaceless spaces, its strange passages of elongated time, the Babel of its voices and petitions that come to see a vision of the global marketplace, a planetary meeting-place. "The white zone is for loading and unloading of passengers only. No parking." I took off from LAX to go to North Korea, Tibet, Easter Island, and often what I saw in the long gray corridors of the airport matched anything I saw at the other end for strangeness and poignancy and affect.

This is the chronicle of only a few these days, perhaps, but a number that grows larger with every passing day. I spend 40 days a year in airplanes and airports, which could come to eight years of my life, if I live long enough; my friends in business or computer-related industries spend more (ten years of their lives in a place they never stop to think about or look at!). The curious, sometimes chilling reality of the modern world is that we spend much of our time not in A or B but in the passage from one to the other, in the empty spaces between.

I felt a shiver of recognition, therefore, when I found out that Zoe Crosher was charting the very same altered space and displaced reality – half weirdly anonymous, half weirdly intimate – that I had tried to record: the sudden thrill you feel when, in a foreign jungle, you meet someone who knows the layout of your hometown. But jungles and hometowns are all mixed up these days, and home may be the state of motion, jungles the line

01 LAX Radisson
2001

of high-rising hotels along Century Boulevard, leading to LAX. The names of the very streets around the airport, Airport Boulevard, Aviation Boulevard, World Way, enforce this sense of living in allegory, a few stories above the ground. Airport Boulevard, Aviation Boulevard, World Way. The post office, taking up a whole block, never closes.

The photos I grew up on gave me glimpses into an exotic world of transport and wonder; they showed the snowpeaks of the Himalayas, customs of the Amazon, and the vast, primordial spaces of Africa. But now there's a new kind of exoticism coming upon us, which creeps up on the soul and enters our system like the air in a pressurized cabin. A place of random lights and look-alike rooms, of friends (of lovers) whose names you don't recall, and windows that offer the sight of people taking off into new lives. It's not a comfort at all to

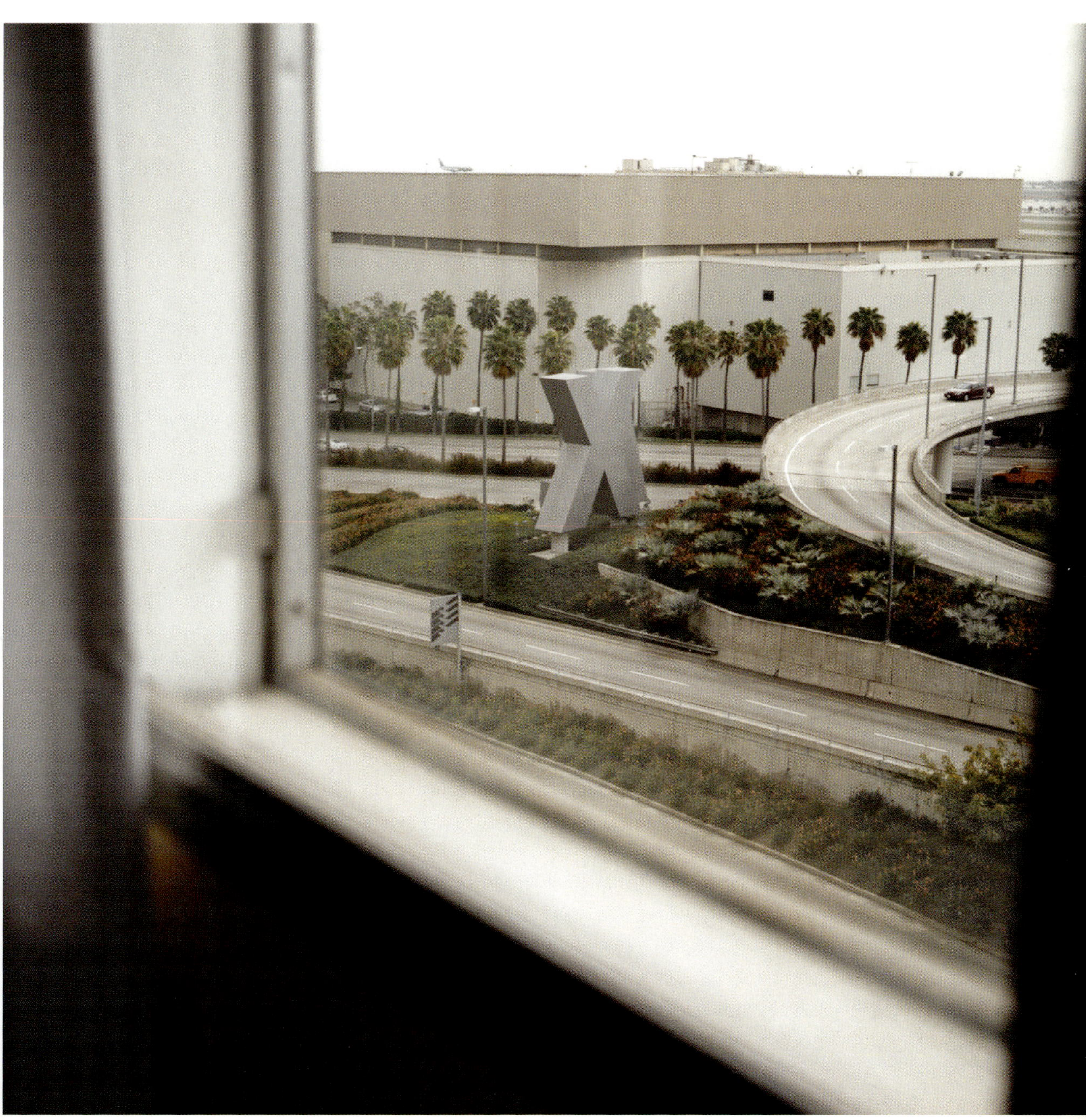

02 LAX Courtyard by Marriott
2005

be riding those moving walkways in concourses exploding in fluorescent light, but it is a comfort, sometimes, to know that someone has been there before you and tried to make it intelligible.

I have stayed in the Motel 6 on the wrong side of the 405 freeway near LAX. I have slept in the lobby of the Sheraton, and enjoyed free overnight parking at the Thunderbird. I have watched the lonely drinkers at the Proud Bird bar listen to air-control instructions on their headphones while watching planes land and take off again. The Theme Restaurant, which looked like a forgotten relic of the Space Age when I stayed at LAX, is now called the Encounter Restaurant, and looks like tomorrow's piece of pastiche.

Zoe Crosher's work starts off at LAX, but takes us somewhere very different, to that global

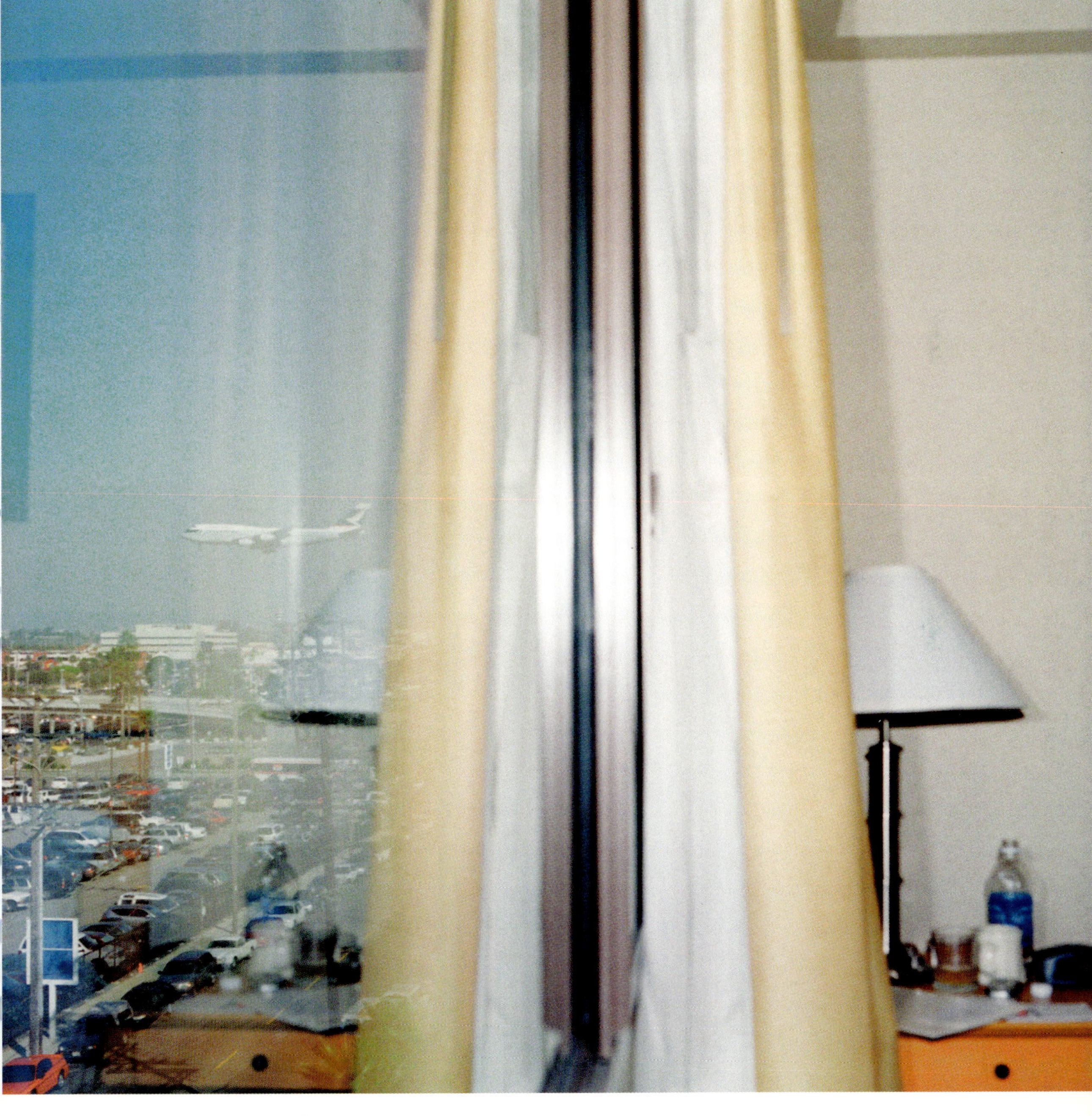

03 LAX Sheraton Gateway
2001

Airportland where the billboards are all for Korean companies, the words "hotel" and "taxi" are understood by nearly everyone, while a stranger is walking towards you with a smile and an extended hand. You don't know who he is, but he has ideas about you; and when the light comes up in the morning, you know you're in a place you don't recognize, but you don't know exactly which of those places it is. It gives me heart that she is going off, ahead of us, to map this unknown country, fearless as one of the explorers of the 19th century, investigating India or the salt flats of Utah, and ready to risk herself, even to lose herself, in the process. Like all art, her pictures teach us how to pay attention.

– Los Angeles Airport
July 2005

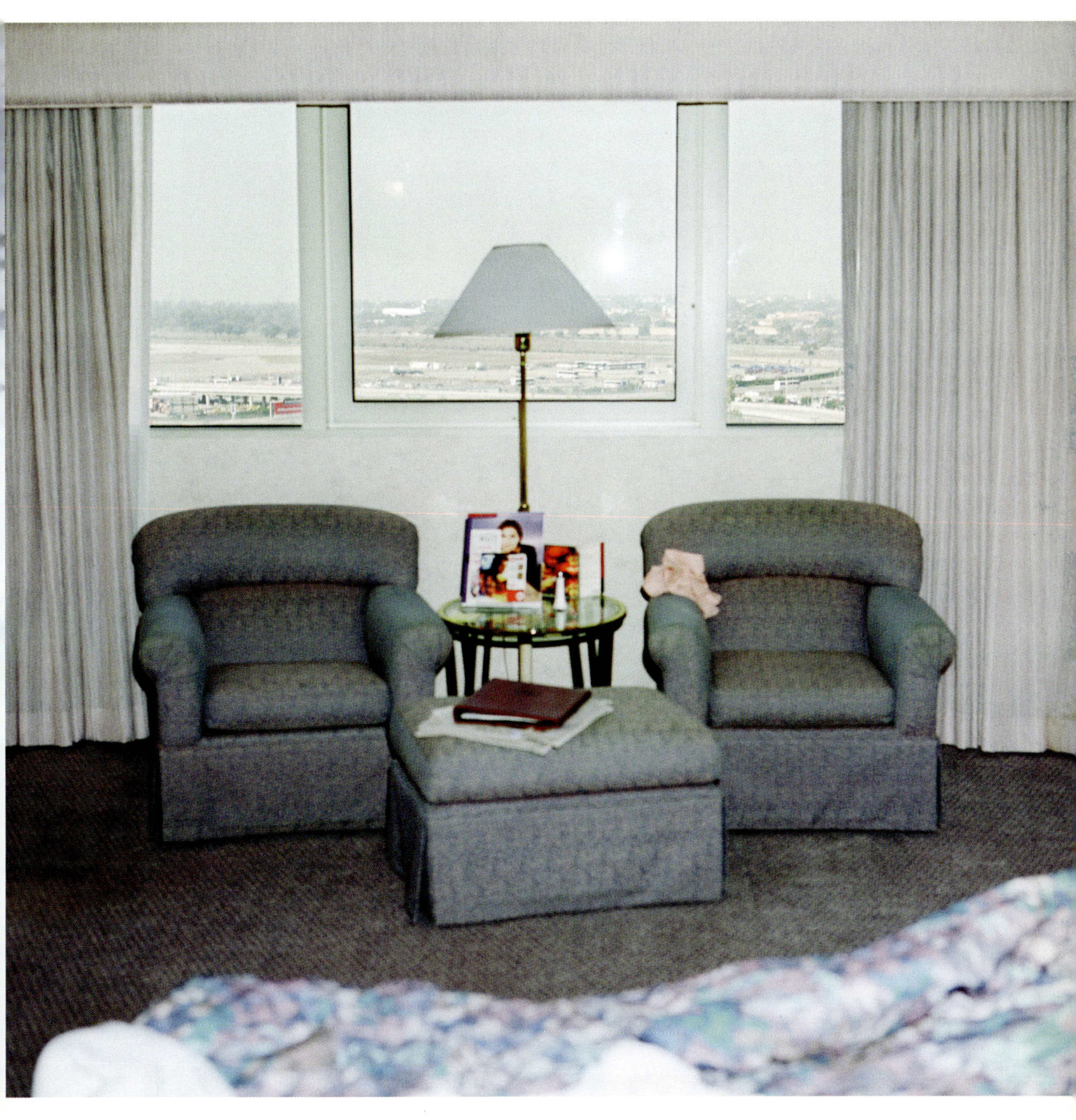

04 LAX Crowne Plaza

2003

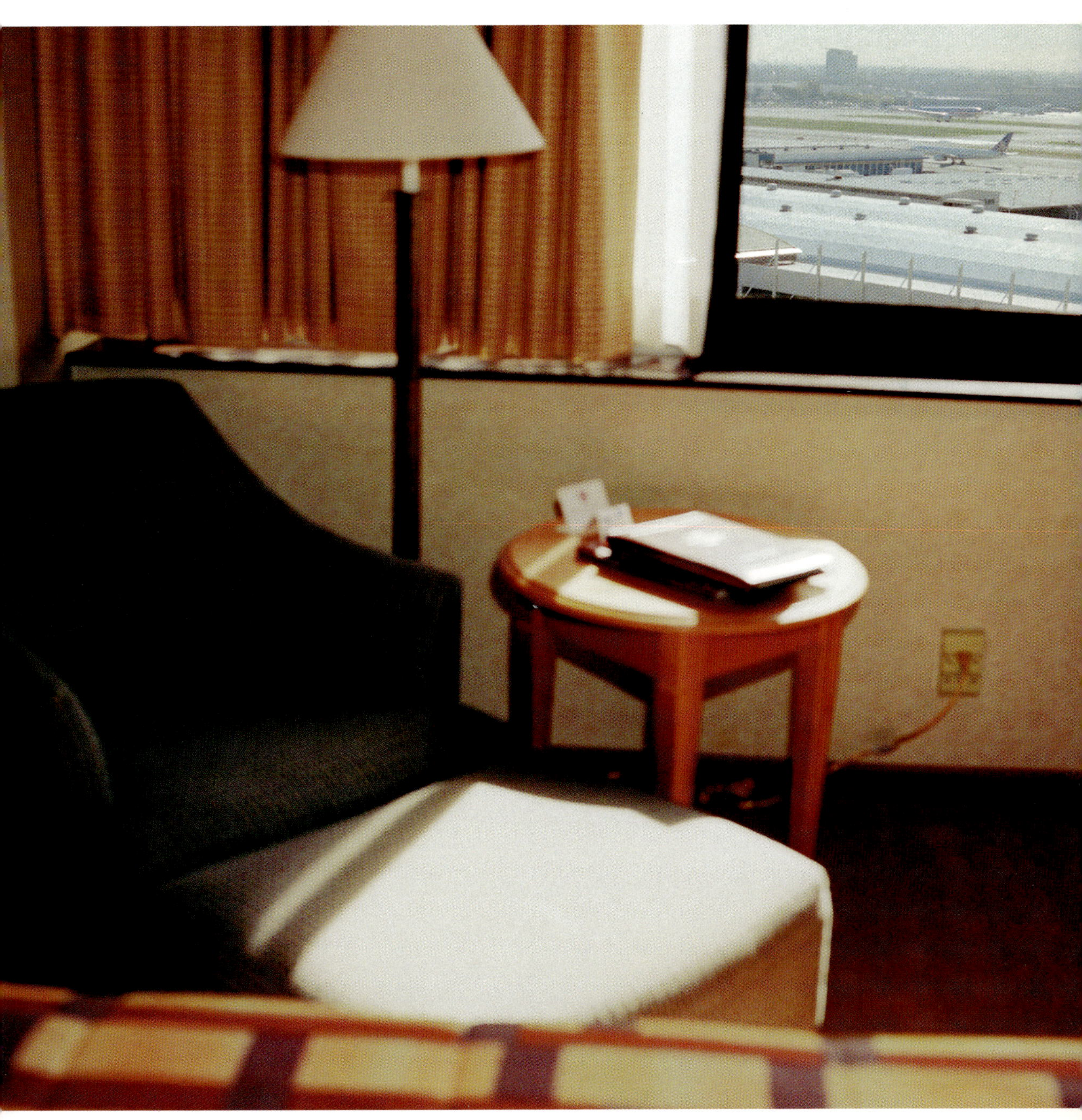

By Norman M. Klein

14 WAYS TO NOT SEE THE AIRPORT

When the blackbird
flew out of sight,
It marked the edge
Of one of many circles.

Wallace Stevens
from "Thirteen Ways
of Looking at a Blackbird"
Orig., journal Others (italics),
Dec. 1917, pp. 109-111

I.

In the world of the airport, perhaps more than any other stop in our globalized civilization, we never leave, only arrive.

Let me explain with a simple test case, then take us through thirteen other ways to *not* see the airport:

Tomorrow morning, I fly out from Burbank. Like an adventure in good medication, I plan to *not* notice many things. First, my departure gate will have no distinguishing scars. It will be a dead ringer for a hundred other gates at the airport. Next, the flight pod (my seat) may be taking me to Singapore, for all I know.

After takeoff, I enter hibernation. For three hours, I ignore the velocity, turbulence, even the distance itself (as stewardesses have been told for generations: for travelers, the less said, the better. Act like they're on a boat in the middle of a bathtub).

At last, having never quite physically – or even mentally – left Los Angeles, I finally arrive in Colorado. I leave the pod, to creep along on, as if in an endless pupa stage. The arrival terminal surprises me for thirty seconds. My gate at Burbank has been teleported to Colorado. Everything still basically looks the same. Perhaps I never really left.

Then a nuance emerges. The food concessions and the newspapers are different. That restores my sea legs. Refreshed, I look for the van to the hotel, to a chain I already know.

For decades, the Howard Johnson chain, on post stops throughout America, had the following embossed on its paper napkins: "The best surprise is no surprise." Similarly, Orson Welles is reputed to have said that in Los Angeles, all roads lead to airport. This world where we never leave has been promised for a century at least.

My flight turns out completely different, quite wrong. From Denver, I take a creaky prop plane over stiff, dry winds, into Aspen. With gas prices so high, the airline has stopped using gas-guzzling jets for short flights, and recommissioned these clunkers instead.

The air conditioning barely works at all. Air currents are erratic outside as well. Our cabin heaves and twists, even occasionally moans. A glass of water bounces out of someone's hand. I feel as if I am

05 LAX Renaissance
2004

on a bus in the Yucatan. The stewardess tries to calm us with a standup comedy routine. Her eyes are a milky blue, as if she has just been crying. She does a pantomime about an oxygen mask suddenly dropping from the overhead. "Oopsy," she explains, dangles it for a moment. "After you stop screaming, simply place this over your mouth…"

A moment later, "It is so unlikely that we will land on water." She reminds us that we are over the Rocky Mountains. "But just in case, your seat turns into a flotation device, which you can keep with our compliments."

Later, I learn that all this is quite normal in August. The era of high tourism has indeed ended since 9/11. Nearly every flight has a comic melodrama these days, in the era of no food, no amenities, and the risk of endless

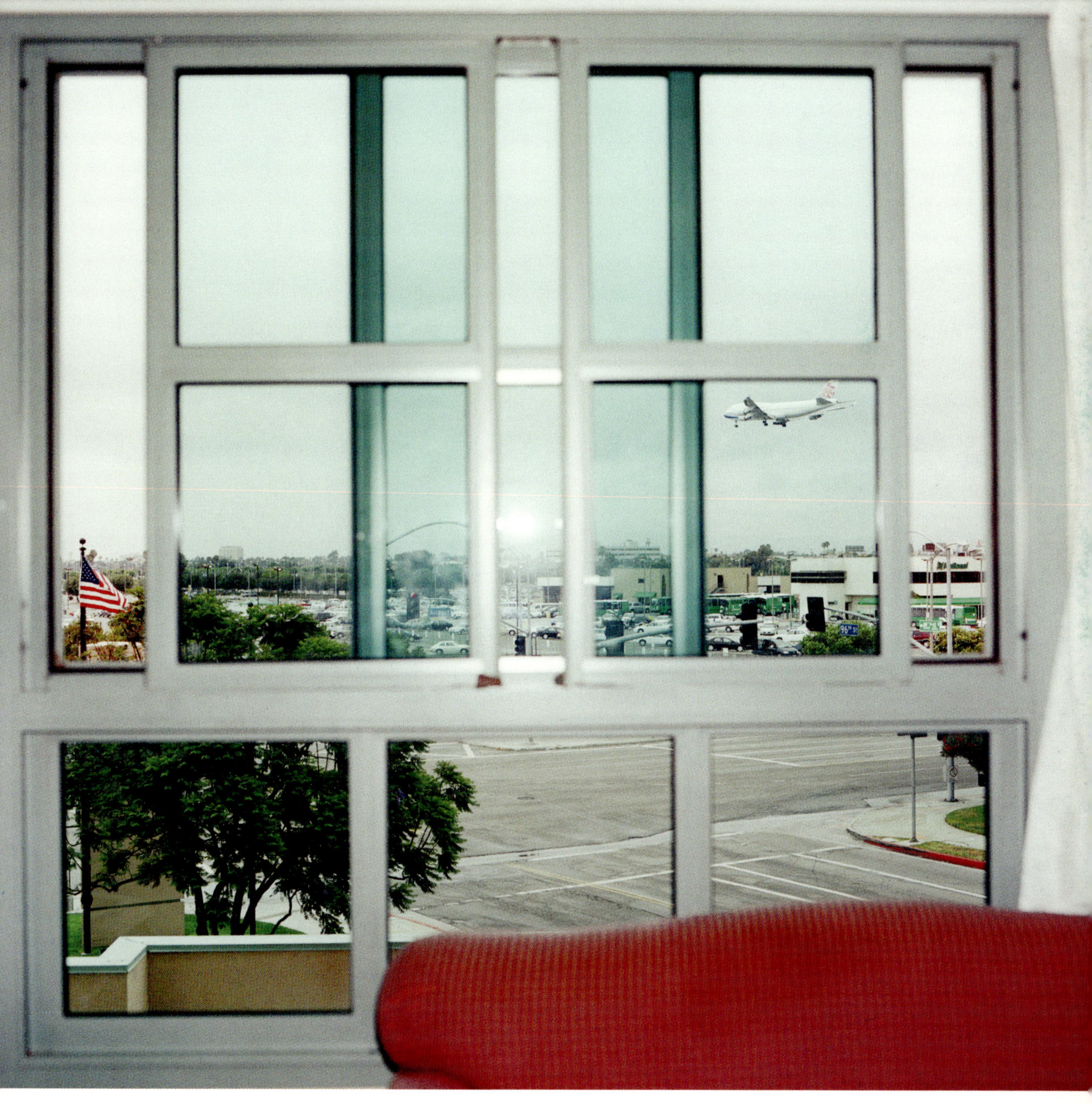

waits. Ten people miss their connecting flight while a guard opens the luggage of a German tourist who is quintessentially not a terrorist. First the guard snaps on rubber gloves, then for twenty minutes, he checks if the man's underwear and socks are about to blow up. Welcome to the twenty-first century airport.

II.

This month, I am researching the Imaginary Twentieth Century for another DVD-ROM novel. With my co-researcher and partner Margo Bistis, I am finding hundreds of ways that floaty air travel was promised since 1850; and stifling TV news since 1878; and unstable teleportable cities since 1890.

Circa 1890: Hundreds of flying blimps before the invention of blimps. Plump bourgeois ladies

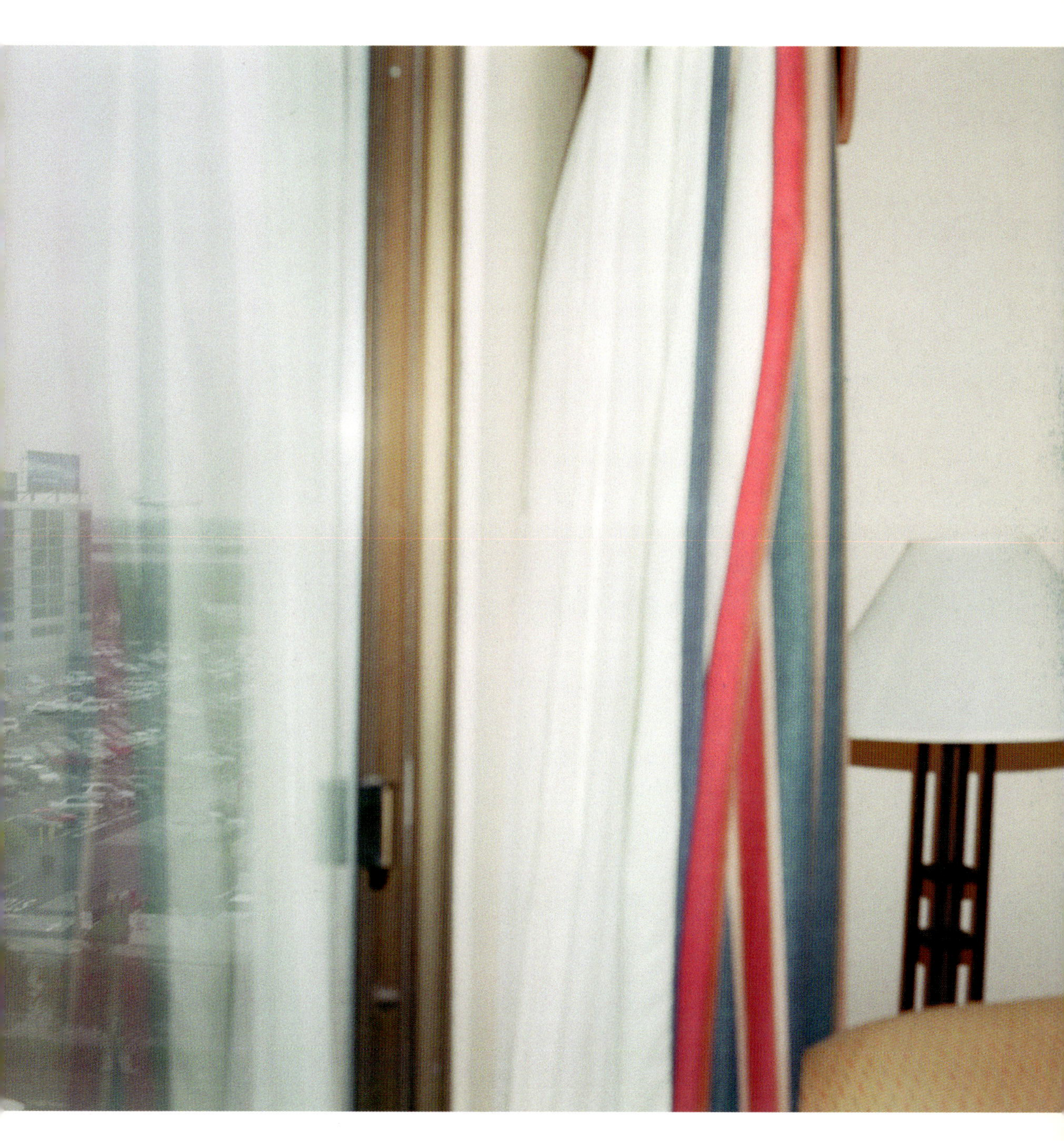

07 LAX Embassy Suites
2003

flirting in the air on the way to the opera a hundred years later. Flying auto-gyros with wings harnessed to businessmen. Blimps shaped like fish or shaped like ocean liners, filling the sky like moths and giant hawks.

Circa 1920: Airplanes circle mile-high imaginary cities. The fantasies of aerial warfare have been realized during World War I, but now, increasingly, they are imagined as warfare on other planets. H. G. Wells imagines nuclear warfare from the air. But most of all, it is assumed that the city of circulation will extend to air travel.

III.
1939: Inside the New York World's Fair, at the Futurama exhibit, the imaginary city of 1960 has an airport floating on a pool of liquid.

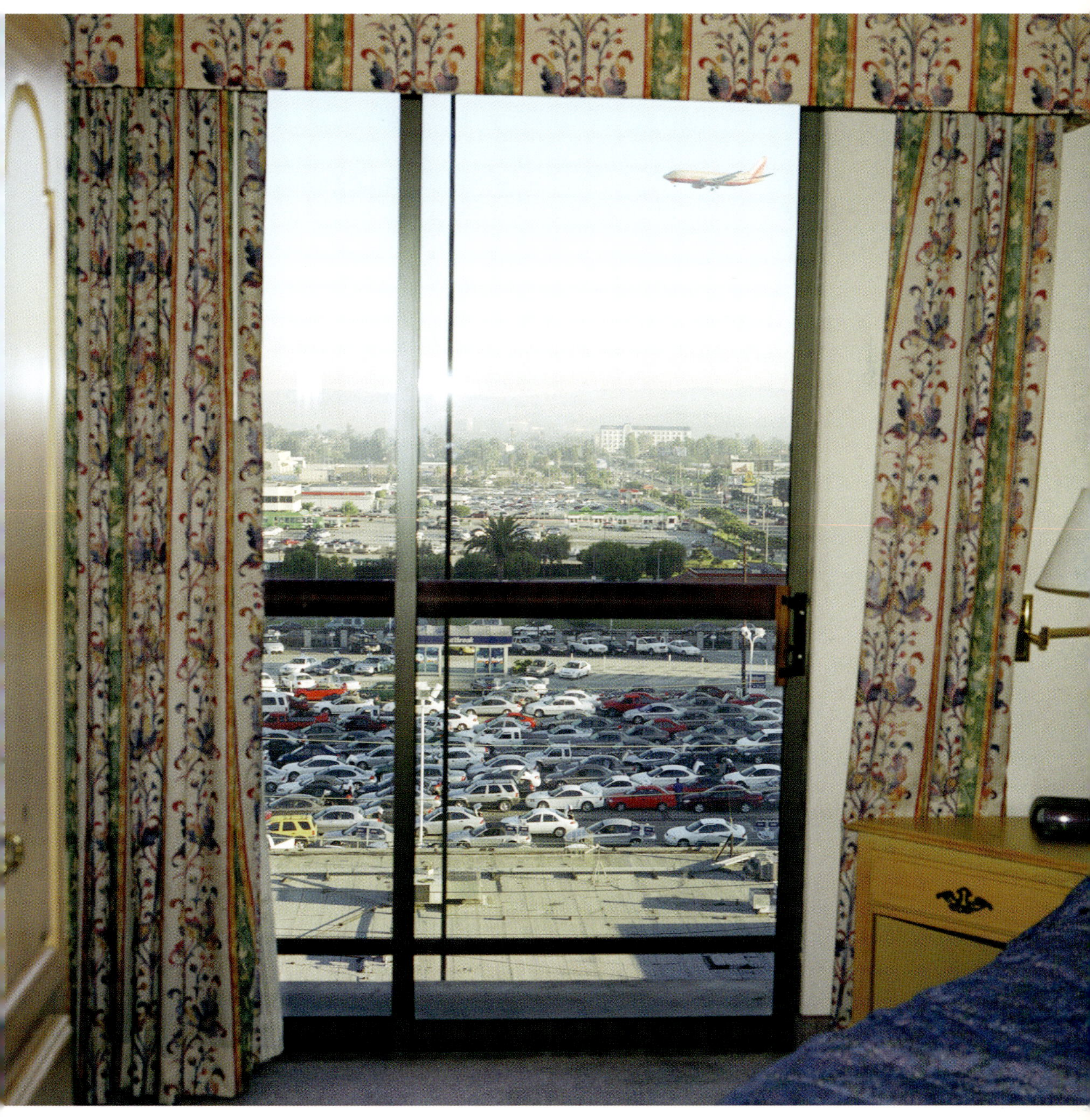

08 LAX Marriott
2003

IV. The Recirculating Window
In the late nineteenth century, the train suggested simultaneity. That is, witnessing the past, the present and the future along three windows. And the differential between the immediacy of the road whistling near the train, and with the experience of seeing it crawling along at a distance. But today, that sense of speed is quite normal and not at all shocking. We email to three countries, while on the phone to another country. It is so fast that speed is now closer to instantaneous, not simultaneous time. That is what Virilio suggested, in writing about the airport decades ago, about a place where you essentially never leave, only arrive.

V. How To Become a Tourist In Your Own City
From cities to accessories, our civilization is obsessed with privacy (more layers between us

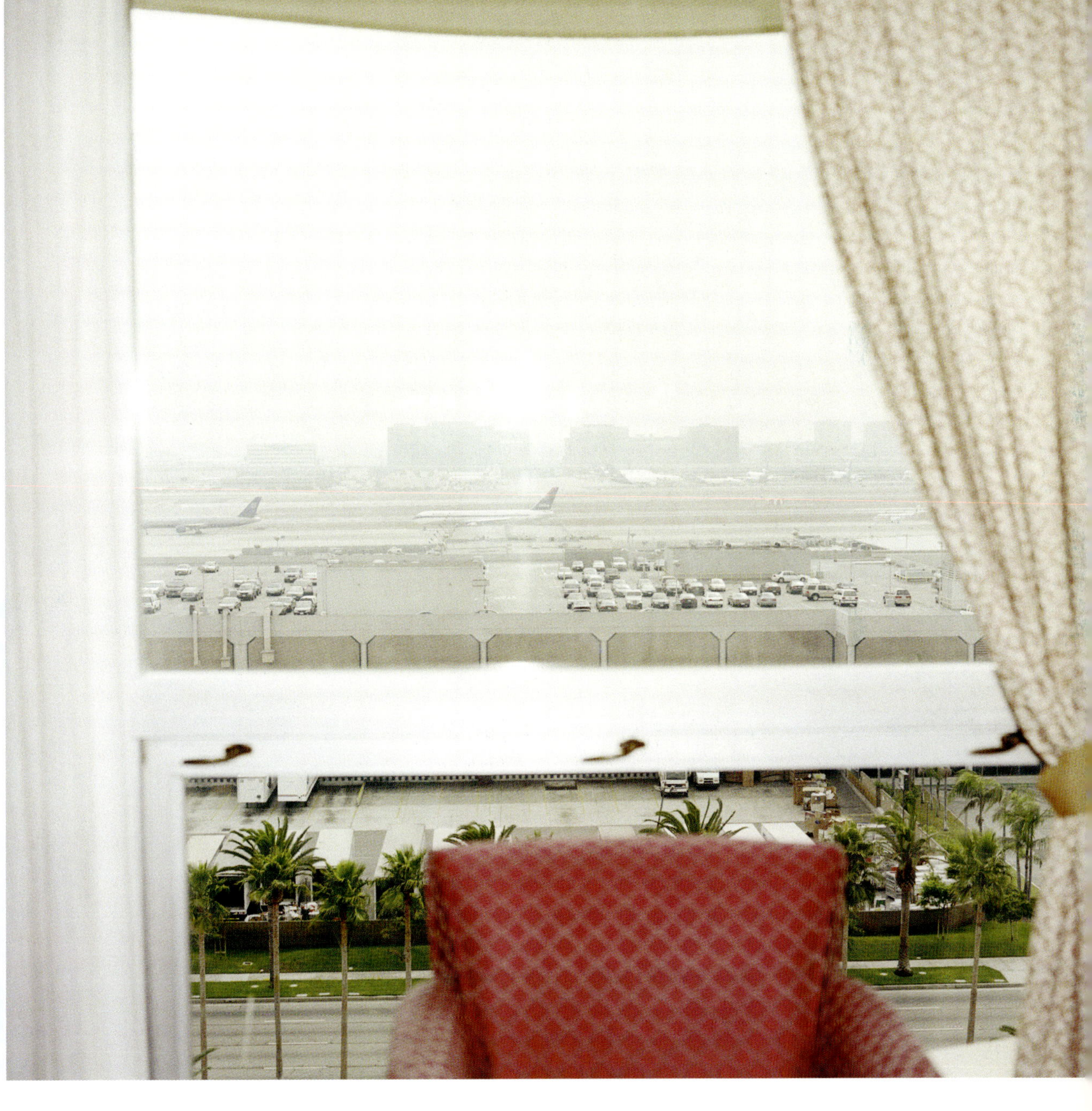

09 LAX Hilton
2001

and the rest), but incapable of much intimacy. The recirculating ironies of air travel remind us constantly.

To live in a space between; to reinvent one's mental map almost daily – and do that cheerfully; that is what seems to be expected. We are indeed being hollowed out, mentally outsourced, and turned into tourists in our own cities, and in our own bodies.

VI. How To Become a Tourist In Your Own Body
Flying is obviously a kind of virtuality. That is, some of your senses are displaced (like the sense of movement). You are sensory deprived. You adapt and compensate. Suddenly your sense of touch becomes very heightened. You feel the sweat on your palms, inside the gloves. Then you feel all the sweat left by

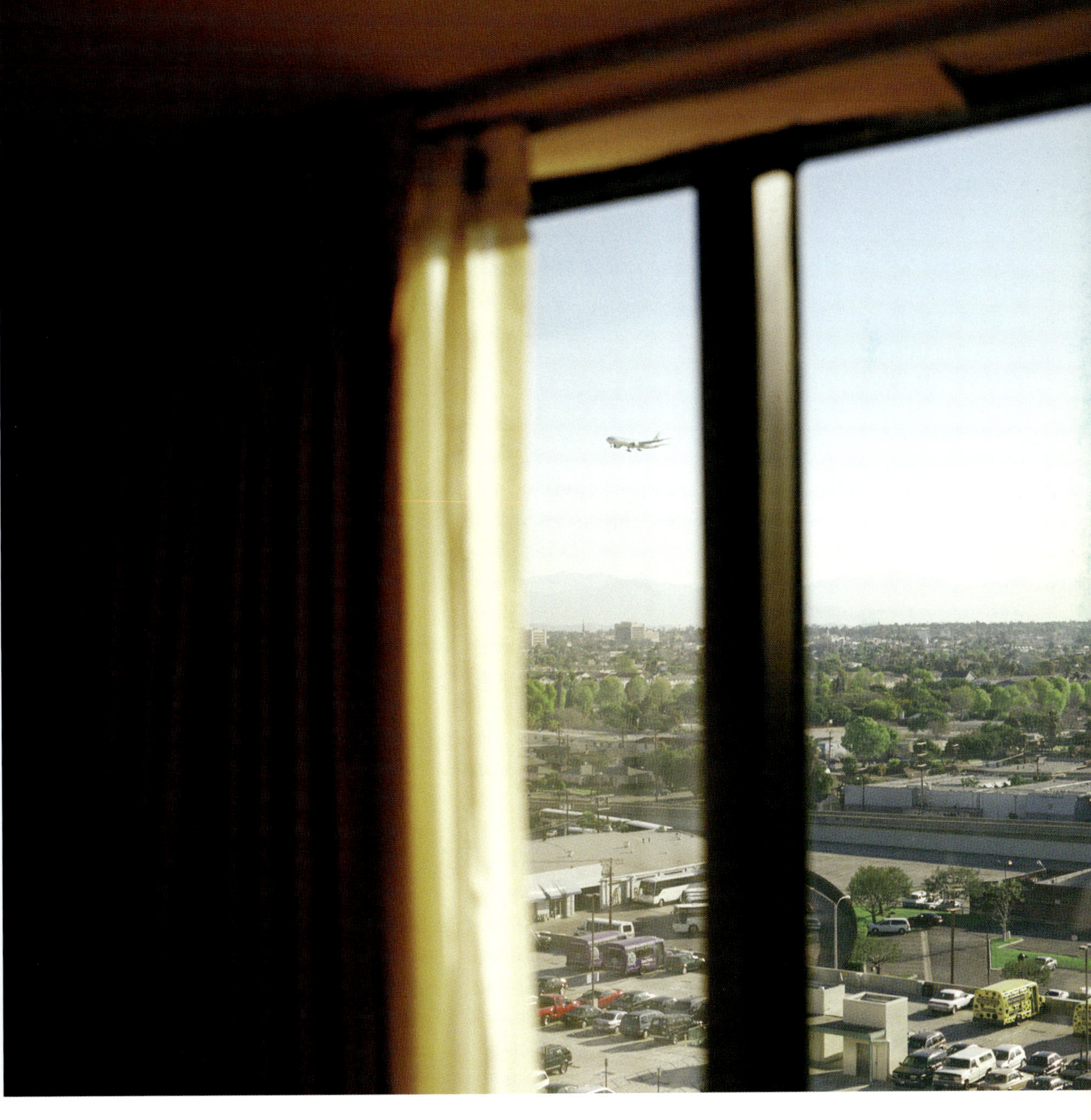

10 LAX Travelodge
2004

everyone else who wore these before you. We are steadily being invaded, hollowed out. Finally, like a parrot circling the living room, we visit ourselves, after we have our face and body rebuilt. The face looks familiar, like a close relative.

VII. A Room For the Night

Artists like Kippenberger – or media critic/ artist Lev Manovich – have turned hotels into a cultural statement. In Manovich's version (in his DVD *Soft Cinema*), the hotel is a stop between airports, the evacuated sense while going through a car wash.

Nietzsche also lived mostly in hotels. It is a longstanding modernist tradition. Today, its distractions are often compared to living with only your cell phone as your address.

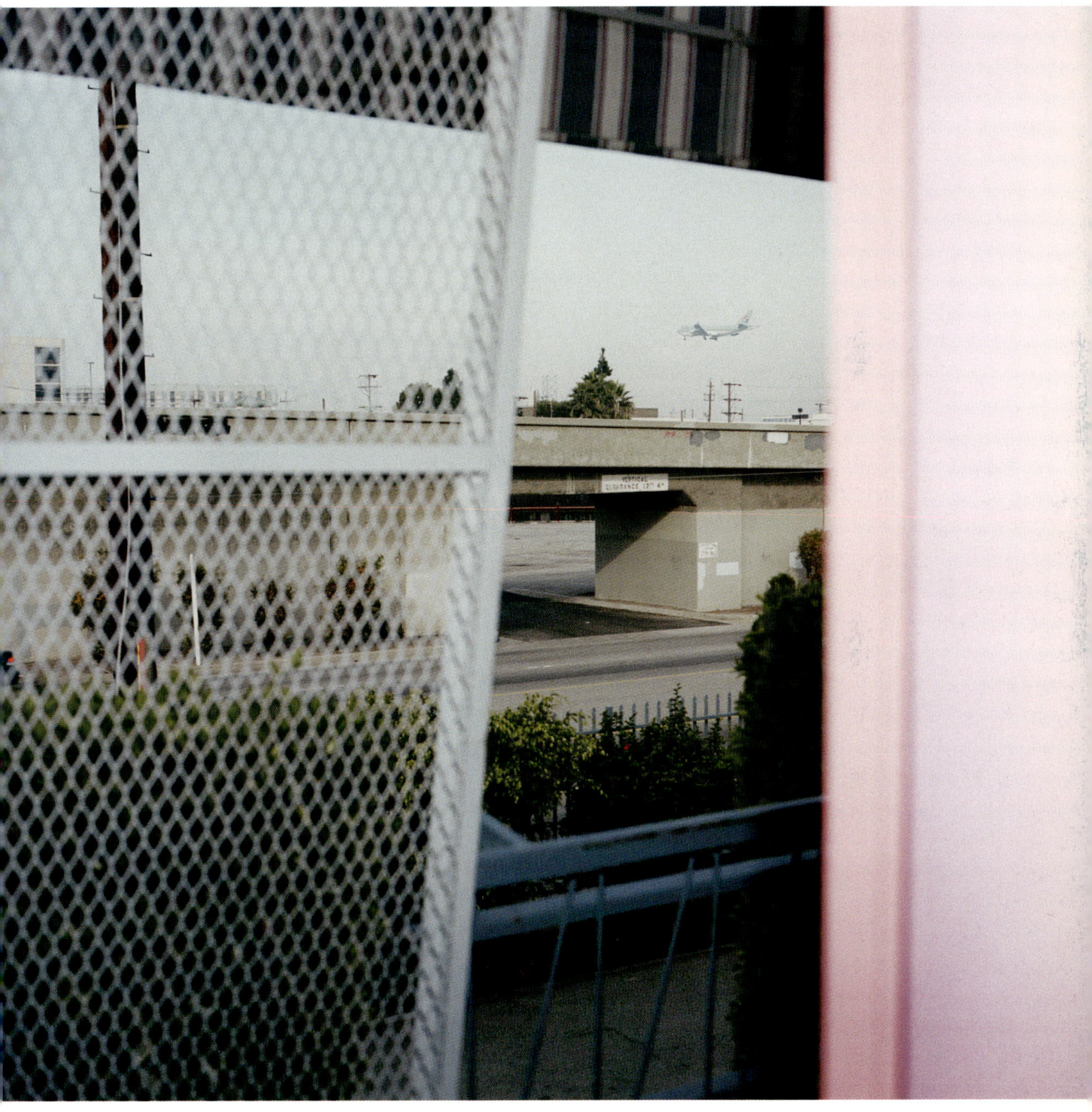

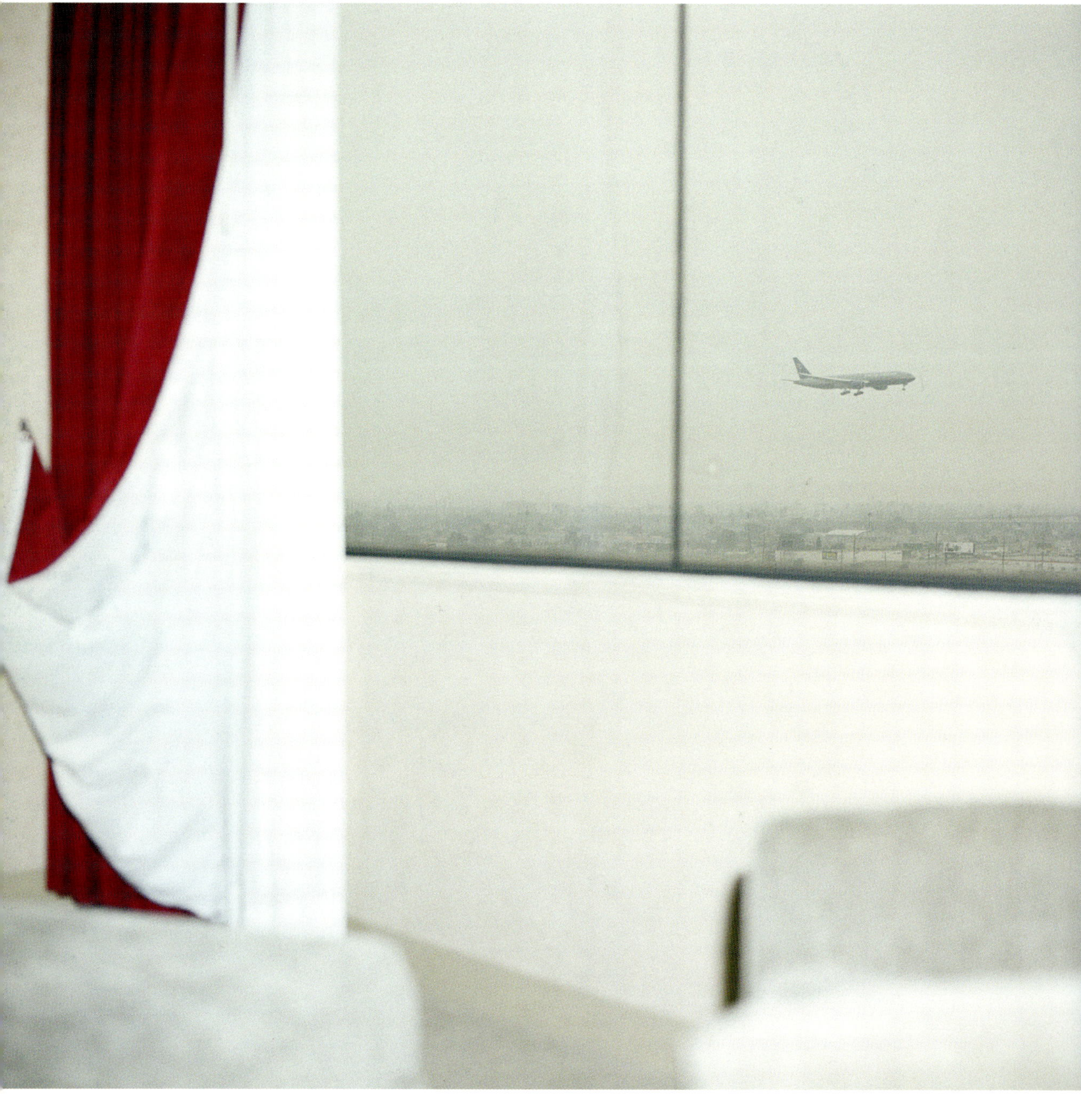

VIII. Homeland Rule: Stations of the Cross at Airports Since 9/11

11 LAX Westin Hotel 2003

I watch a guard put on his vinyl gloves. Very scrupulously, he unfolds a man's underwear packed inside a suitcase. Nothing blows up. The owner of the suitcase, as unlikely to be a terrorist as is humanly possible, waits for twenty minutes. They check for bombs inside his rolls of socks.

Strange to remember when airline travel was the metonym for globalized living, for brisk comings and goings. Now it is a symptom of a senior moment for America, or should I say, an adolescent misunderstanding. An old American aphorism: After the horse escapes, you double-lock the barn.

IX. Cities As Airports

In the nineties, architect Hani Rashid designed a city directly inside an airport. As he – and

12 LAX Quality Hotel
2003

Lise Anne Couture, his partner at Asymptote – later explain:

The airport is today a surrogate city-space equipped with all the attributes of urbanism yet at the same time hygienically insulated and controlled. The advent of digital technologies has spawned in most business sectors three seemingly contradictory trends: long-distance communication by sophisticated electronic means, and a vast increase in travel and the need for face-to-face meetings. As businesses merge and grow around the globe, airports have attempted to keep pace by offering executive business areas, lounges, places of worship, and a plethora of other features that at one time only real city space might have provided. These trends suggest that airports will transform into places that people not so much simply pass through but instead use and inhabit. Cities have historically evolved around trade routes

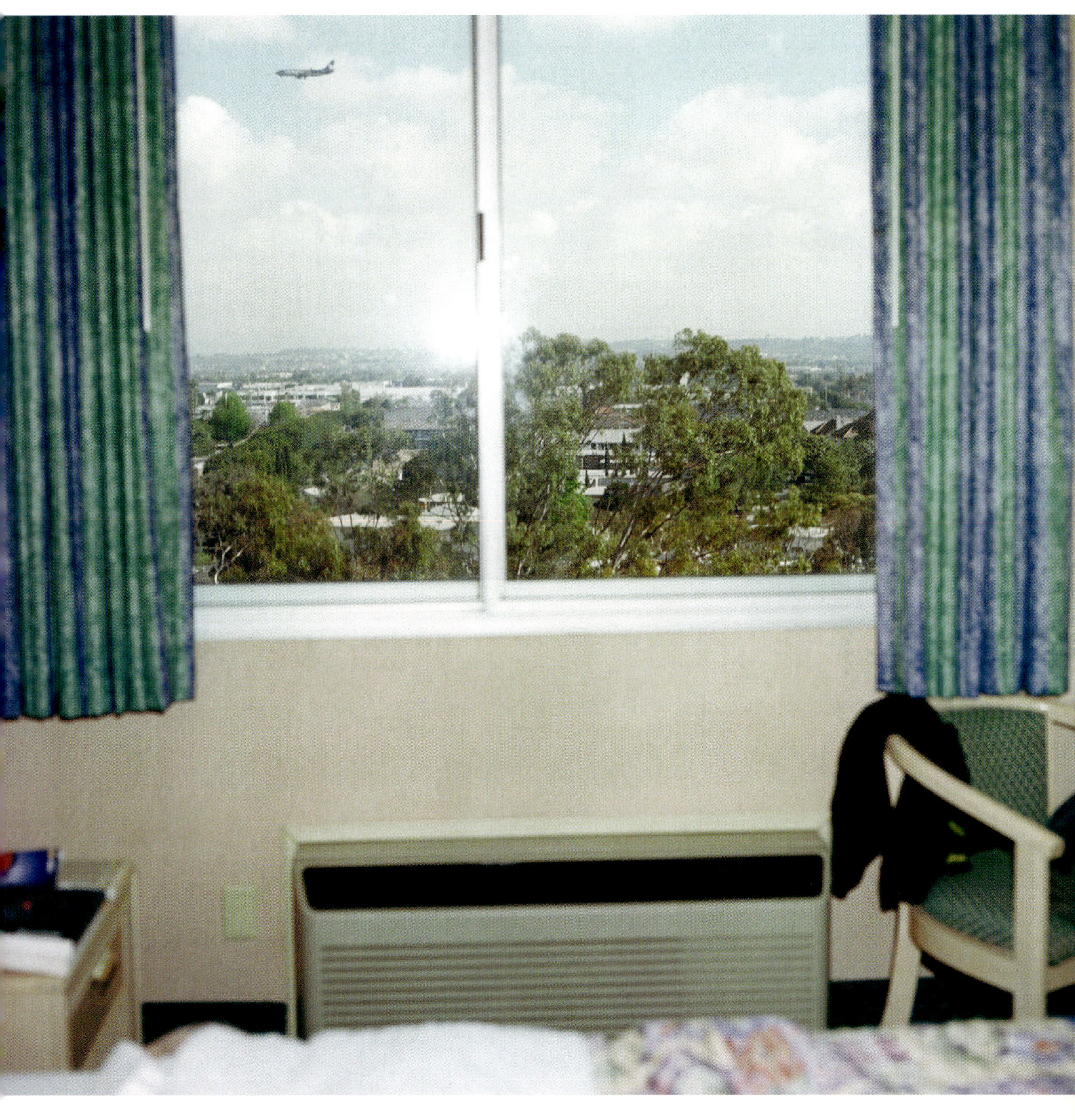

13 LAX Holiday Inn
2002

and transportation nodes, including waterways, highways, and rail lines. In today's continually changing global corporate culture we are seeing the evolution of city space occurring in close proximity with – if not wedded to – new airport planning. [1]

A splendid fantasy, straight out of plans of 1900 for the future city in the air; but I doubt that this utopian statement is true any longer, not as our crisis grows since 9/11. Globalization is shrinking and localizing space much more now. The promise of living in complete sensory deprivation – up in the air – may be ending. At any rate, the client backed out.

X. My Crash Landing: Indestructible Until Proven Otherwise

In 1987, my flight from St. Louis to Chicago is very rocky. We sense that something is wrong when the stewardess starts to cry. Flight crew rush to the

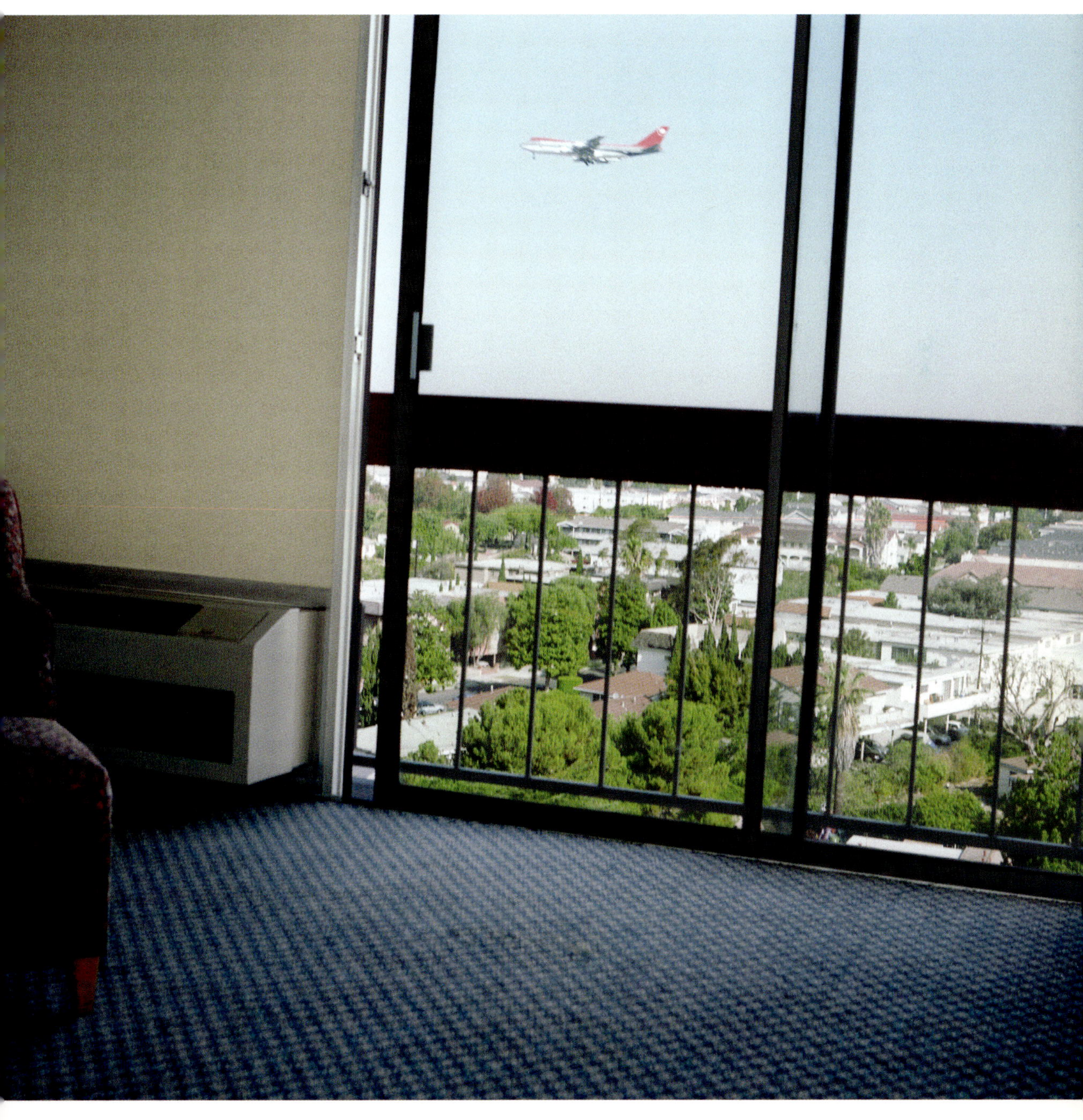

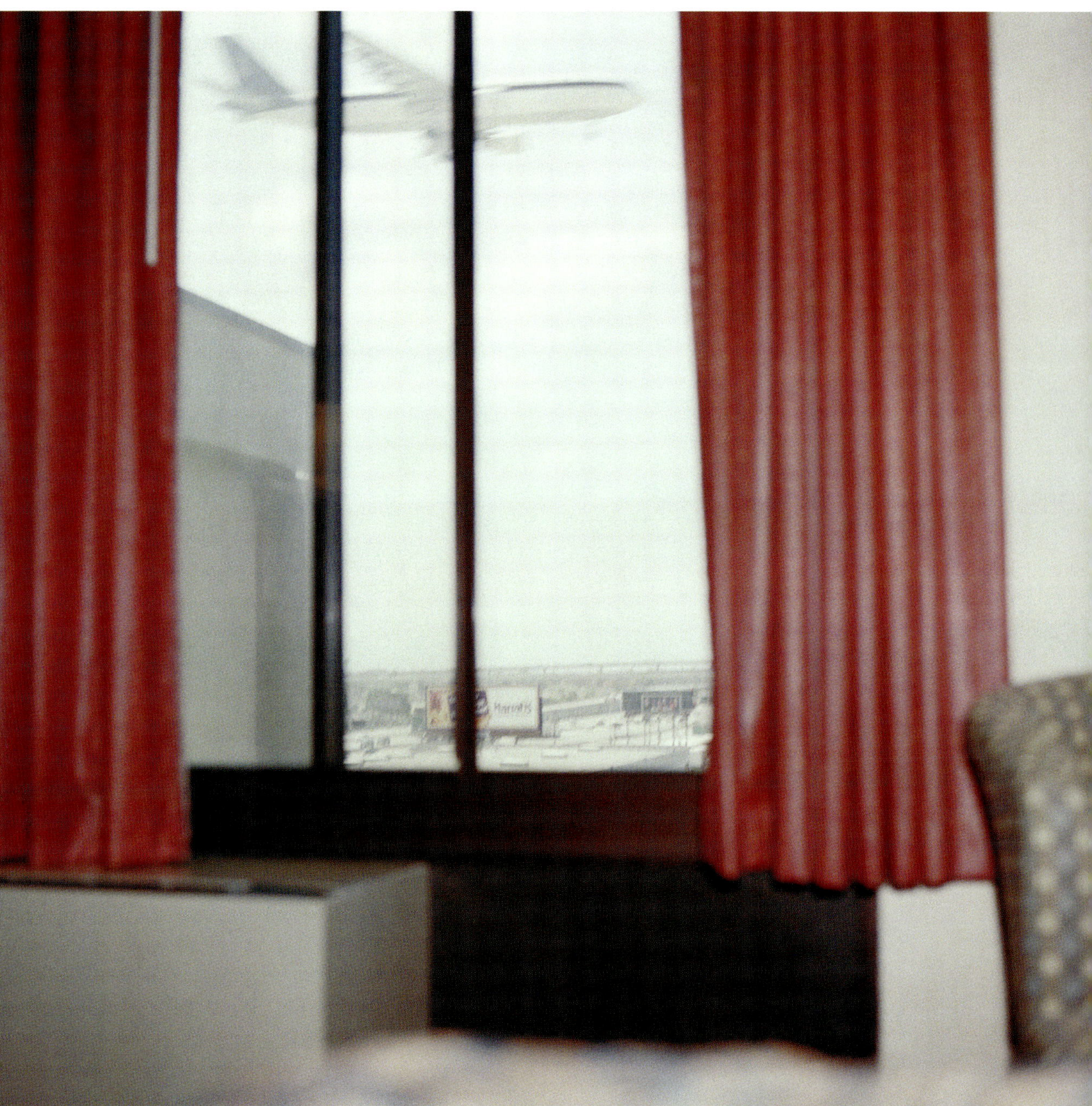

center of the aisle. They tear up the Velcro carpet, and keep yanking at something that looks relevant.

Finally, the captain explains that our landing gear is jammed. "Last month, someone landed an airplane without any windows left," he explains. "I'll get us down."

Not very comforted, we prepare for a jolt when we hit the ground. I fit the seat on my neck, to keep it from breaking. But mostly, I tie the notes for my next book around me, as I lean close to the carpet.

A man watches me, shakes his head. We chat sideways, inches from the floor. "What are you doing?" he asks nervously. "We might die. Die."

"Actually," I answer, "I have no idea how to get ready to die. Which way do I look for an answer? Up at the modeled plastic ceiling? I'm not actually planning to die. Maybe I can eat my way out of the plane." We finally slide on to foamed runway. Luckily, it is also raining at O'Hare. But on the way out, I slide badly down the chute. I sense an extremely fat buttocks sliding behind me, much faster than I could go. I am tipped off, and shred my cartilage.

Weeks later, the surgeon tells me that I will undoubtedly get arthritis in twenty years.

In the spring of 2005, my knee flares up while I am walking (more like scrambling) across the Brooklyn Bridge with my son, who is tall. The swelling begins a bout of arthritis, particularly after I fly to Oslo and back. Up until that week, in response to my near crash in 1987, I used to always say: "I am indestructible until proven otherwise. You want to fly... fly with me. I am statistically

EAST OF LA CIENEGA

LAX Motel 6
LAX Best Western Suites
LAX Comfort Inn & Suites
LAX Hotel Tivoli
LAX Marietta's Inn
LAX Microtel
LAX Caesar's Motel
LAX Topper Motel
LAX Dai Ichi
LAX Sea Breeze Inn
LAX Ramada
LAX Super 8
LAX Royal Comfort
LAX Adventurer Hotel
LAX Econolodge
LAX Airport Hotel
LAX Hollycrest

15 LAX Motel 6
2003

immune." Now I have an autoimmune disease. I guess there can be too much of a good thing.

XI. Special Effects and the Entertainment Economy

Air travel is the ultimate special effect, repeated in hundreds, if not thousands, of films, commercials, TV shows, computer games, amusement park rides. I remember, as a little boy, taking the parachute jump in Coney Island – a shredded remnant left from the 1939 World's Fair. It was over before it started.

But the sense of diving in mid-air is very much at the heart of all special effects in our culture. Perhaps it began with what they used to call switchback rides in the 1880s, then with roller coasters. The switchback was a gravity train on trestles and piers that could wiggle its way

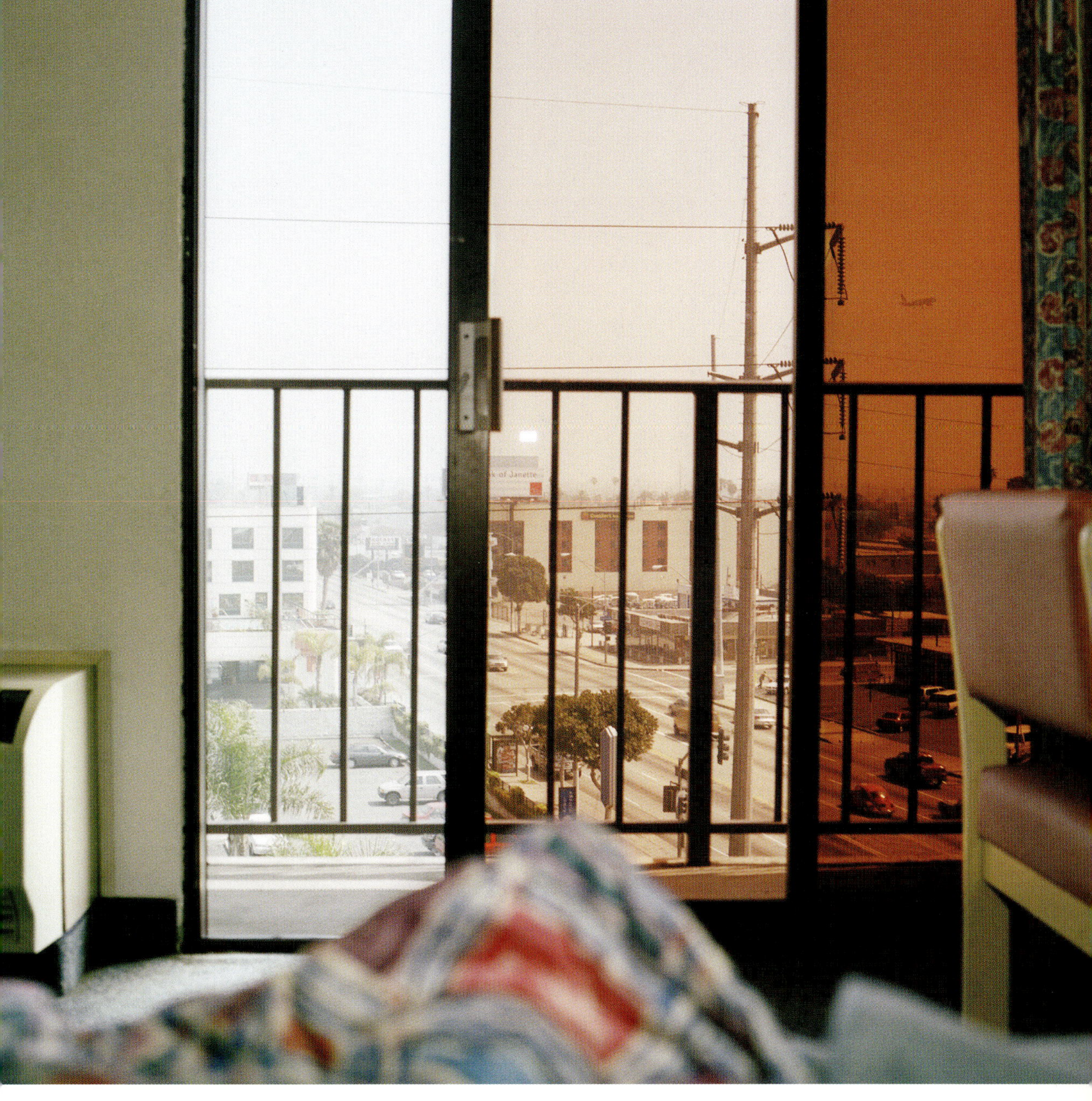

16 LAX Best Western Suites
2003

down a mine shaft. However, trains normally must be almost perfectly level. So the exaggerated switchback became the imaginary railroad crash. You strapped yourself in, and pretended to die. The theatricality was thrilling. Afterward, when your stomach caught up, you had a few hot dogs.

XII. Collective Memory in the Age of the Electronic Baroque

In an era when impulse is industrially engineered as never before in the history of our species – probably an exaggeration, but in the spirit of our hyperbolated ad and branding culture. But even if this is mostly true, how does our collective memory operate when it is engineered? On an airplane, we imagine ourselves rolling on wheels in the sky. We are not supposed to think "forty thousand feet?" I suppose that is as sensible a parallel as any to industrialized memory.

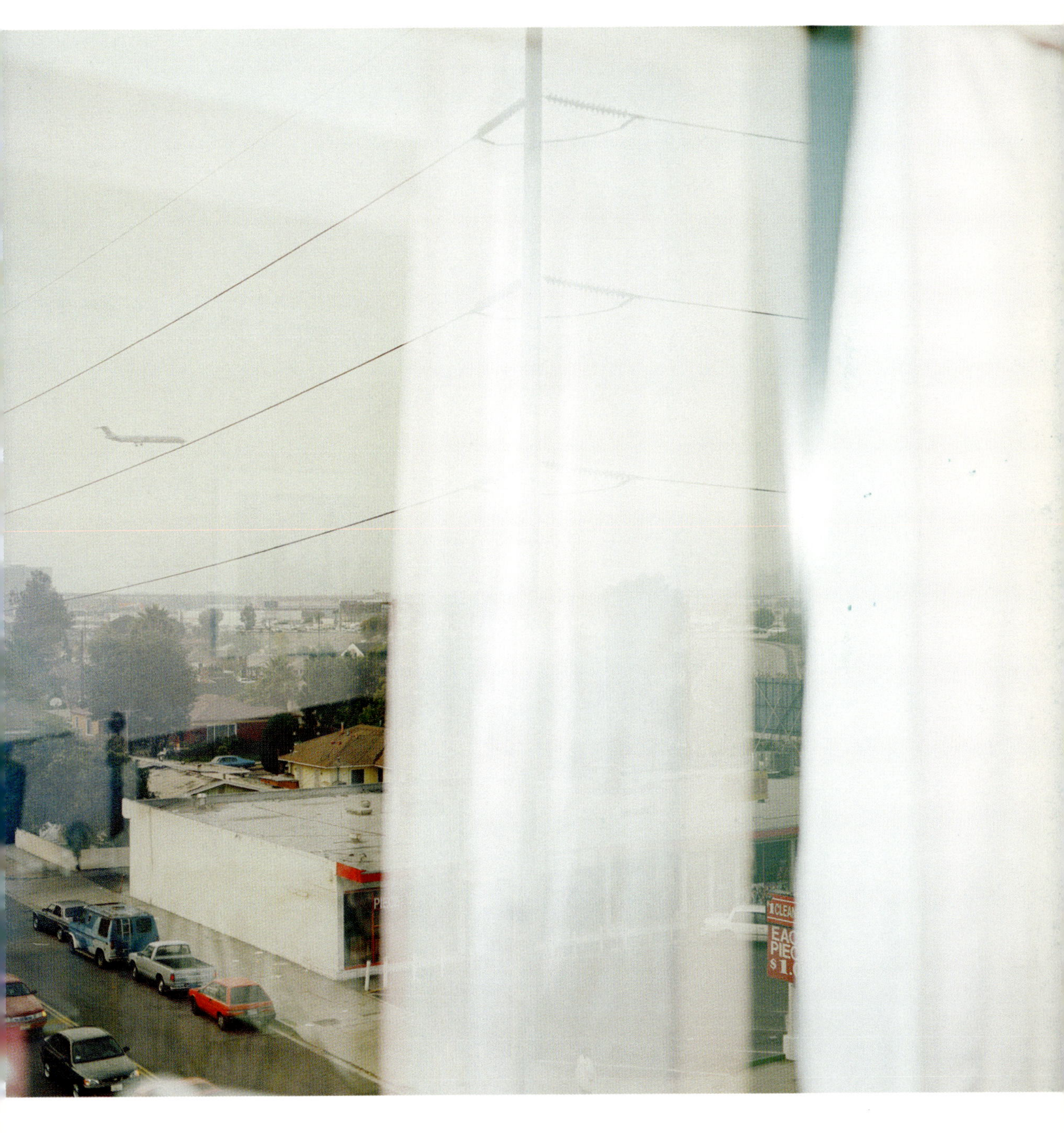

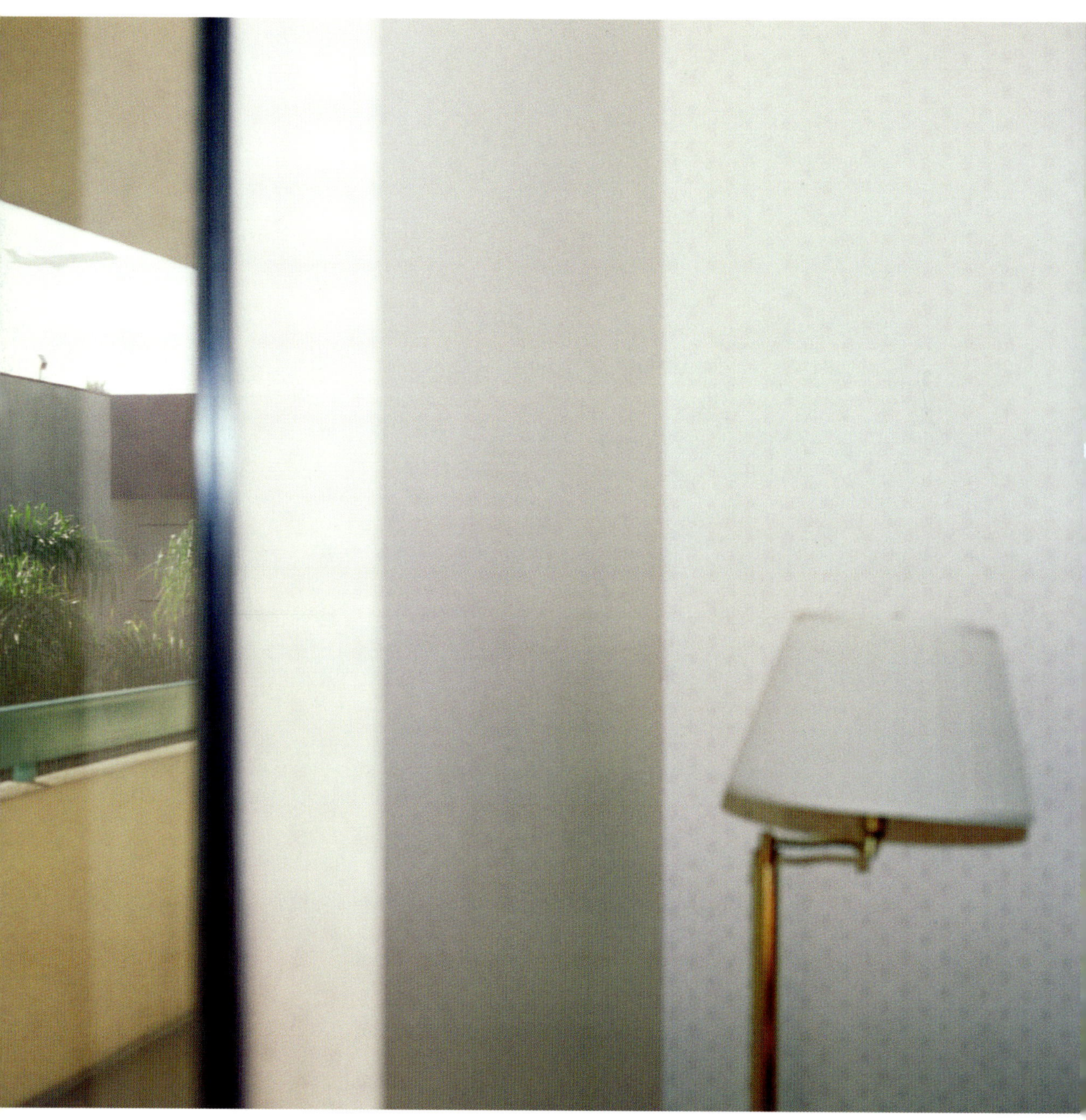

You remember only the hum of the engine, and the sociability that is supposed to keep you happy. We become detached from anything but the service. There are no causes and no teleology. We record more than remember.

XIII. Holding Our Breath (The Ergonomic Way to Flirt With Disaster)
I have never learned how to breathe properly. Yoga specialists always correct my breathing. So I mostly breathe the wrong way, just to spite them. Someone told me once: "The way you live, you flirt with disaster, but so slowly, almost no one notices. With you, it's like waiting in line at the airport."

XIV.
At a literary conference in Berlin, I saw the literary giant Hans Magnus Enzensberger

17 LAX Comfort Inn
2002

translate – into German – Wallace Stevens' poem "Thirteen Ways of Looking at a Blackbird," then reread it in English, with apologies.

It was late at night. I was wilting with jet lag. The lecture and the translation began to hum like an airplane. Suddenly I woke up. Enzensberger was struggling with:

I do not know which to prefer,
The beauty of inflections
Or the beauty of innuendoes,
The blackbird whistling
Or just after.

It is impossible to translate anything properly from one language to another, he explained, even from one moment to another. That is the lesson, that the sound is immaculate. There are no

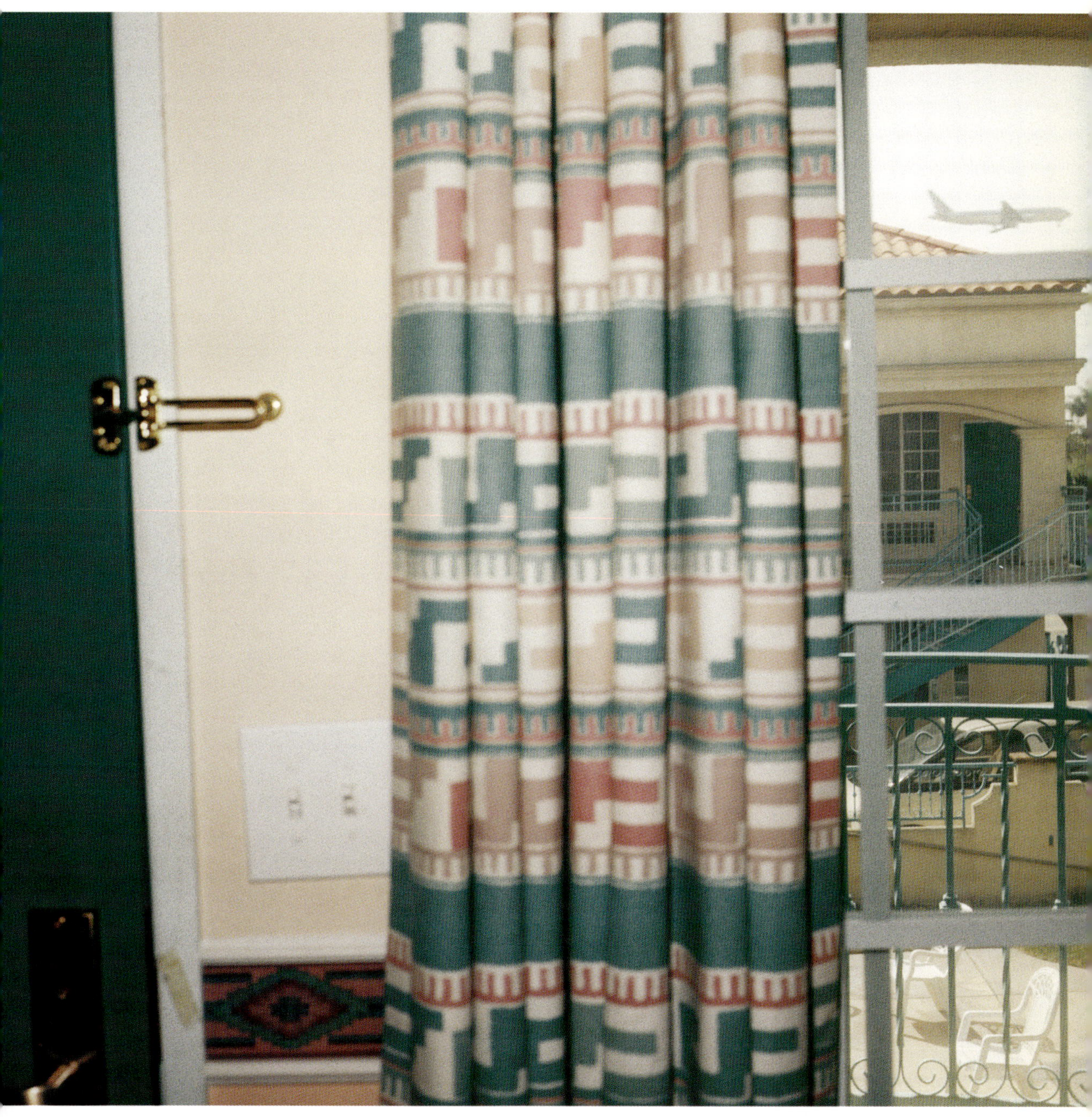

19 LAX Marrietta's Inn
2003

moments when we actually touch down, if there ever were. This is an uncomfortable sensation.

The river is moving.
The blackbird must be flying.

It was evening all afternoon.
It was snowing
And it was going to snow.
The blackbird sat
In the cedar-limbs.

[1] Rashid, Hani and Lisa Anne Couture. *Asymptote Flux.* London: Phaidon, 2002.

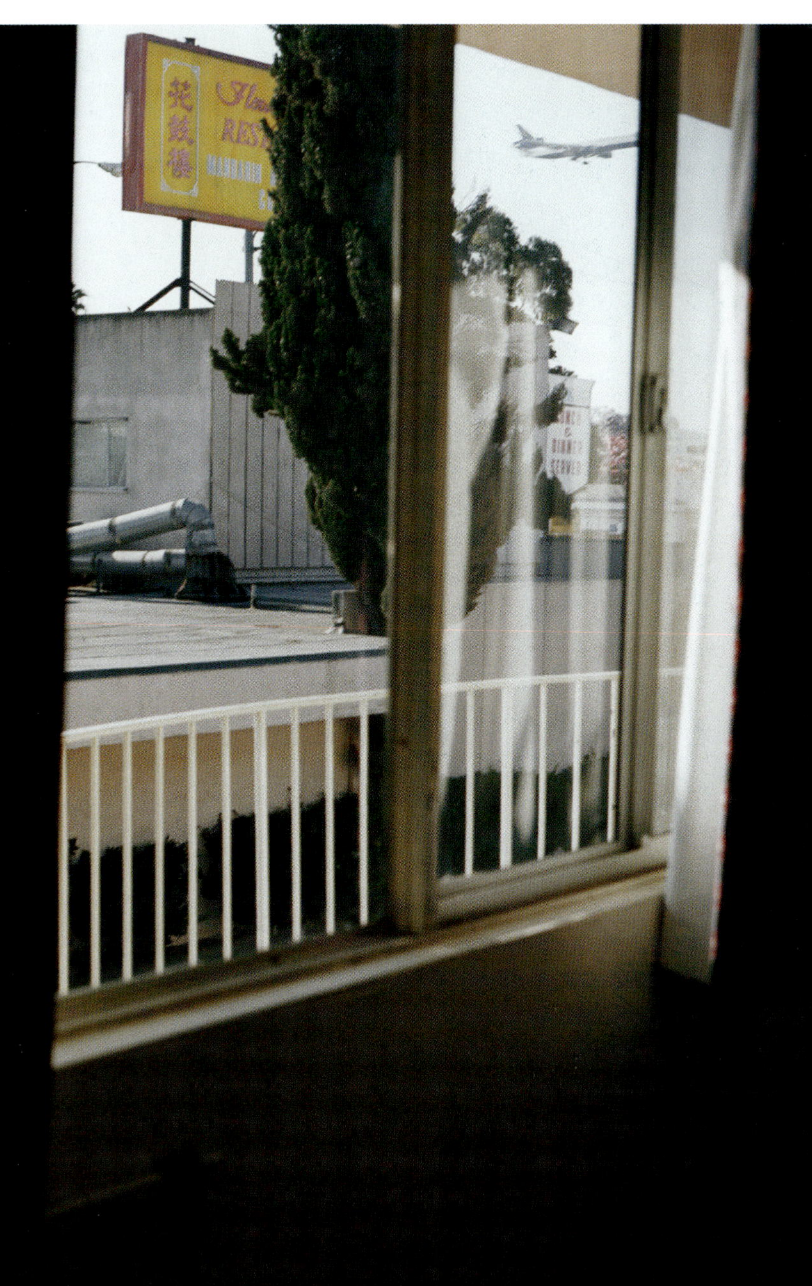

20 LAX Microtel

2005

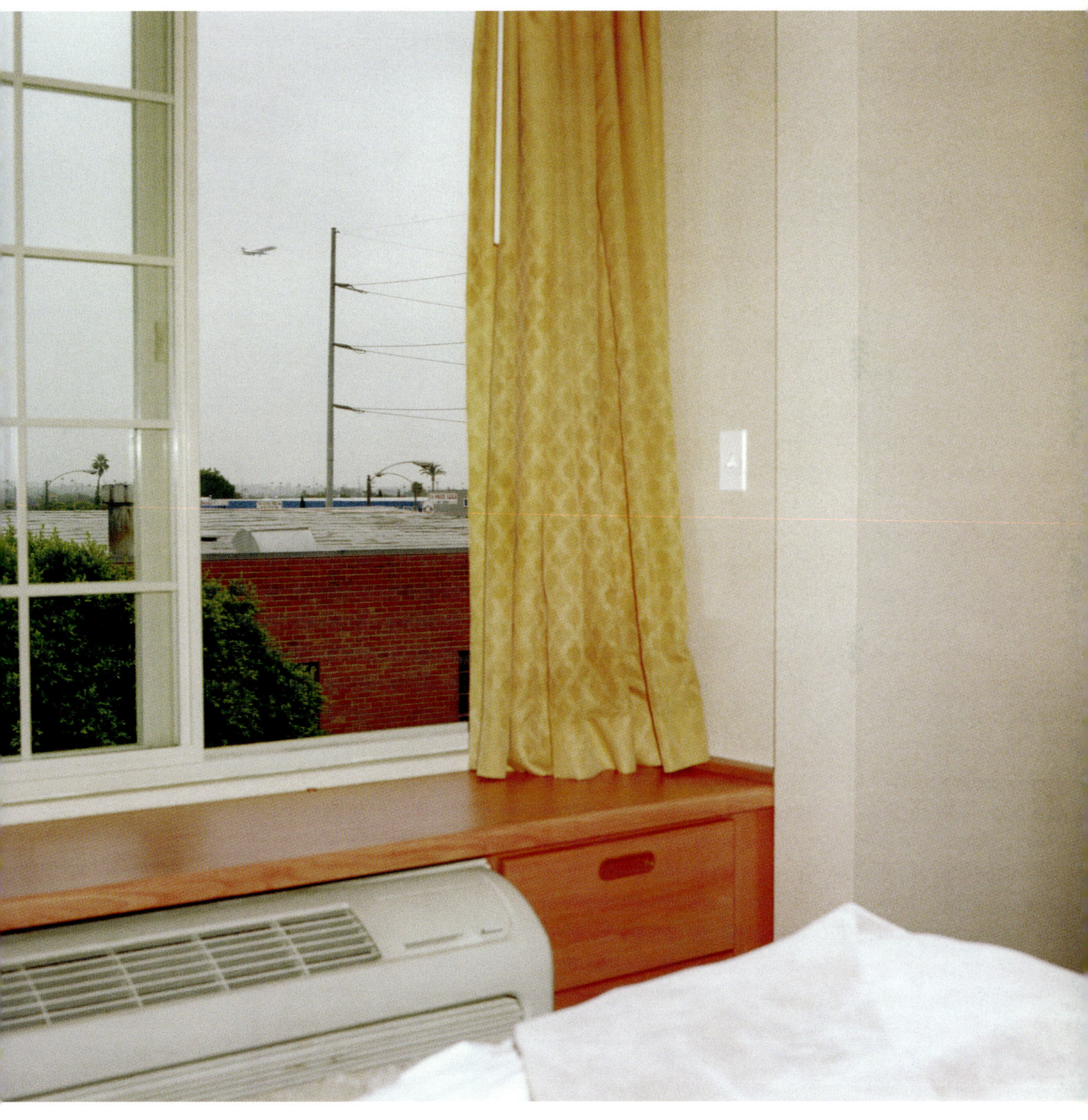

By Julian Myers

ZOE CROSHER: OUT THE WINDOW (LAX)

I leave half-conscious while the morning is bruise-purple; time stutters past, eyes open and shut. I am in the air watching the night retreat over the ocean and then, as if in a dream, I'm in a dim bathroom in Sea-Tac airport. I stay for several minutes, watching the mirror and listening to passengers piss fitfully. I splash my face with water, and then call again. Has it only been six hours? "I'm in Seattle. I'm here." I don't know why I've come, but now I can't go home.

Out the Window (LAX) is a series of thirty-one photographs taken over a period of four years, from 2001 to 2005. Each picture is, in its exhibition size, twenty-seven inches square, the size of a window. The photographs are discernibly of a piece, and share traits of focus and framing across their sequence. The sharp geometry of the photograph's cropped edge is often echoed within the image itself, with windowsills and standing lamps carving up the picture into planes of faded color. There are often great shifts of focus within each frame. The photographer is in a room, but her eye is sharpest in the long distance, looking out through dust-smeared windows and smoked-glass patio doors; this habit of picturing tends to soften the details of her immediate surroundings into a sensuous blur of patterns. It is a look simultaneously alluring and alienated. The photographs work as studies of form, cascades of expressionist off-color structured by the architectonic vectors of window jambs and catwalk railings, though great attention is nevertheless paid to the contents of these rooms, to their hissing air conditioners and patterned curtains, and to the wedges of morning illuminating their shadowy tableaux. These are *Better Homes and Gardens* profiles shot by a modernist, Neo-Plasticist painting brought back home again.

These spaces are not homes, however, but hotel rooms, all from the area surrounding the Los Angeles International Airport (LAX). This distinction is meaningful. There are thirty-one hotels, and so thirty-one pictures, a figurative map of the periphery of the airport. Each photograph is named for the hotel in which it was taken, which gives them blank, descriptive titles that evoke the vanilla poetry of tourist cliché ("Sea Breeze Inn", "Adventurer Hotel"), clunky neologism ("Travelodge"), and class pretense ("Embassy Suites"). The rooms themselves speak this limited language fluently, and reproduce its most naked aspiration: the promise that travel might momentarily free those who perform it from themselves, from the weight of their class, personality, memory and responsibilities. Therefore these spaces are without any distinct character, and approach the character of semiotic

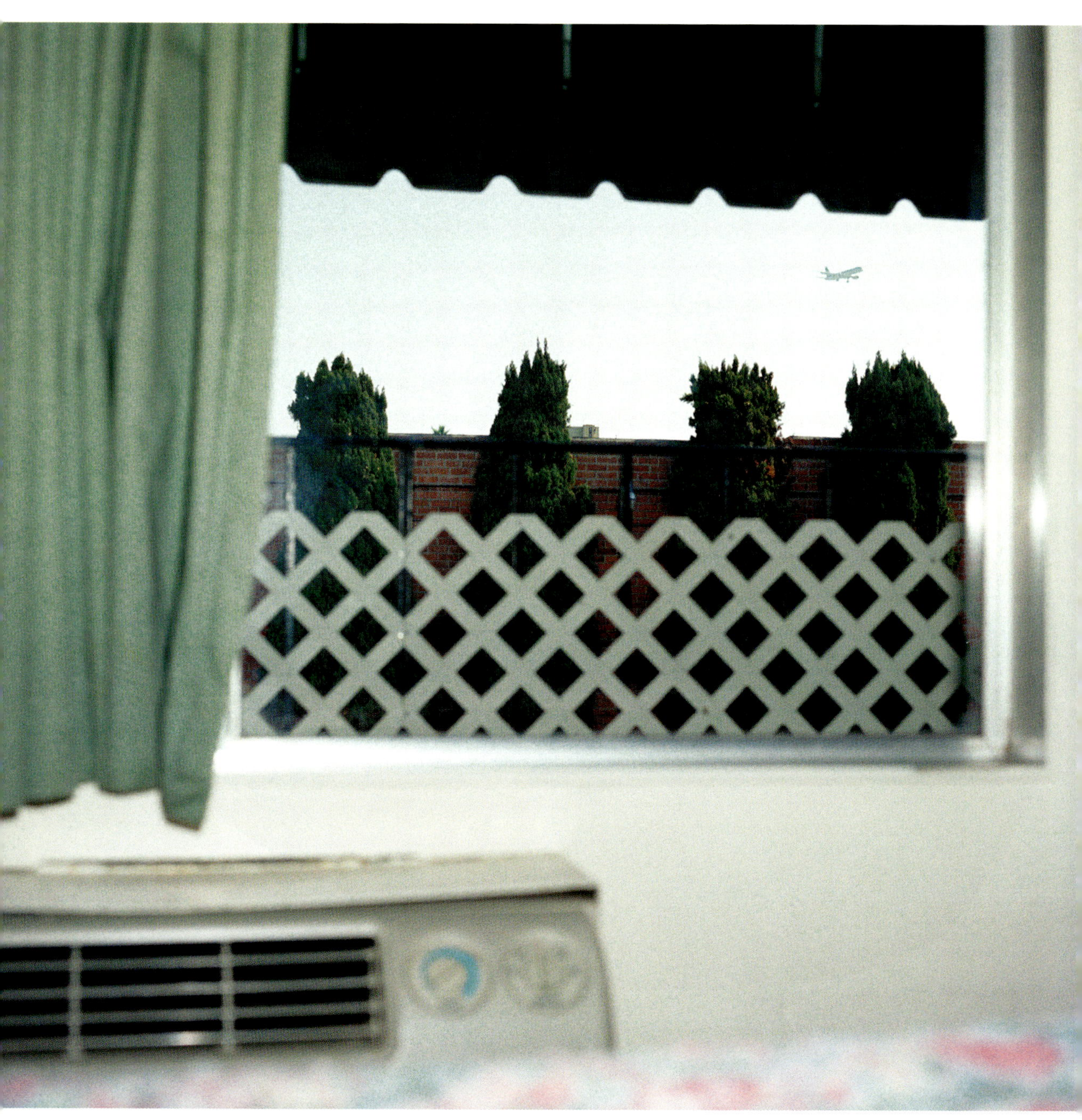

signifiers: beds proffer duvets less comfortable than intending to represent comfort, and shag carpets are less luxurious than designed to evince luxury. Parenthetical curtains are thick, to hold out the light of morning, and generic nightstands declaratively present business cards and lists of cable channels. Plastic-strap deck furniture waits to carve its signature into someone's derrière.

The series has the consistency of a conceptual project, if not the look of one. In his "Paragraphs on Conceptual Art," published in *Artforum* in 1967, Sol LeWitt wrote, "When an artist uses a conceptual form of art, it means that all planning and decisions are made beforehand and the execution is a perfunctory affair. The idea becomes a machine that makes the art."[1] The idea that produced Out the Window (LAX) was simple enough. The photographer would spend the

21

LAX Caesar's Motel
2003

22 LAX Topper Motel
2004

night at the hotel, sometimes with a friend, and sometimes alone. (Several collateral photographs depict these friends, sleeping or standing in the doorway, but Out the Window scrupulously excludes their presence). When morning came, she would aim her camera through the frame of the room towards the airport — the center of gravity around which all these hotels orbit — and press the shutter when an airplane came into view. The camera's focus would be trained on the plane in the distance, rather than the foreground; marks of the immediate environment would be allowed to intrude. The body of work would admit a single image from each site, creating a "basic unit" which, in the presence of the complete series, would offer a virtual map of the LAX hotel belt.

Crosher's method works through the difficulty of taking pictures of Los Angeles, and what she

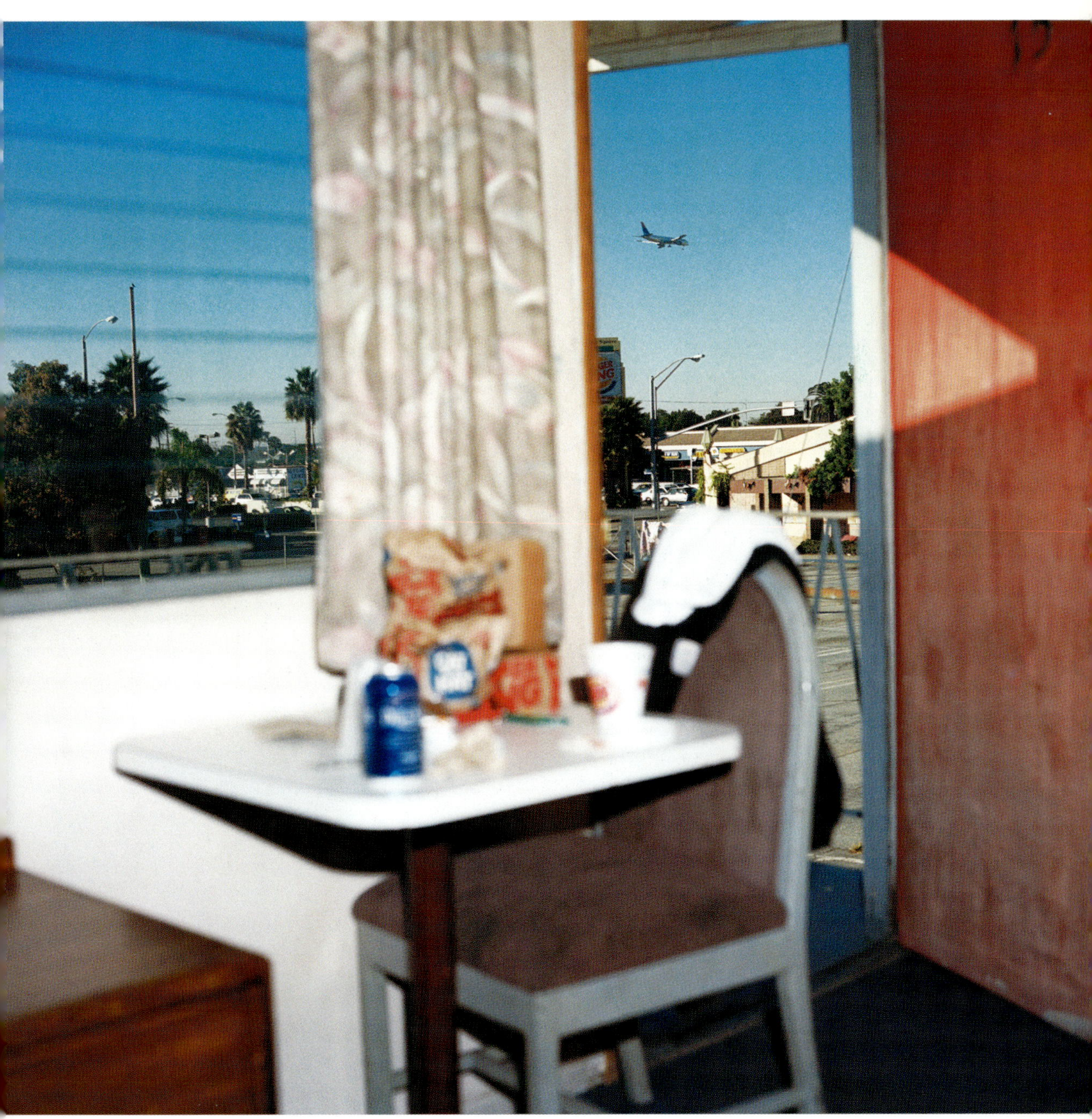

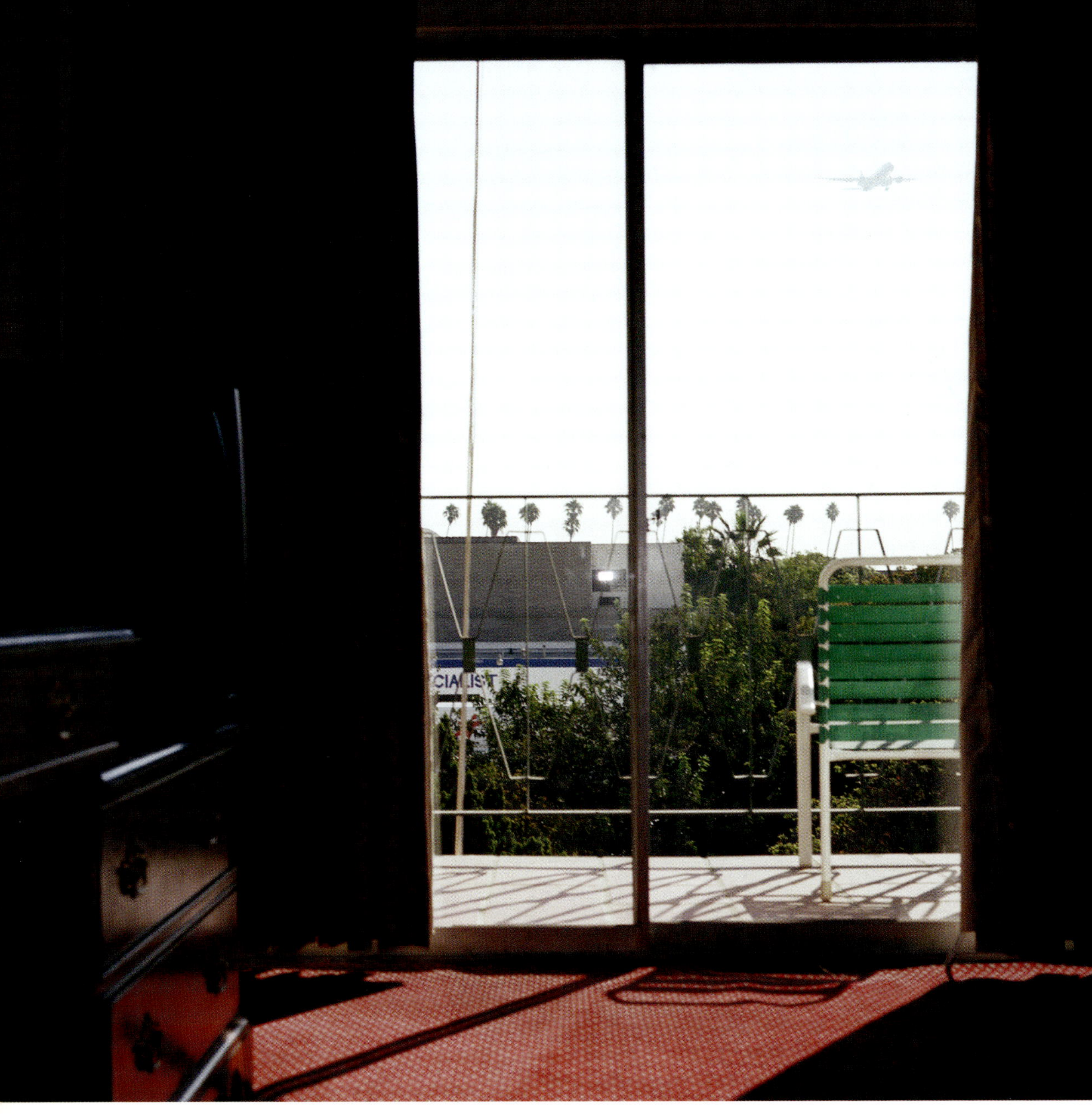
CIALIST

understands as its resistance to being pictured. Photography has typically been understood to be an indexical practice, one bound to recording a certain place and time; LA, however, is best characterized by constant motion, and by the duration of transit. It is a place seen through windows of cars or airplane windows, always while in motion. How should we approach this "place that moves in shifts and perpetual motion, with no real center, no point of concentration"?[2] Her response is to take a sidelong glance at its airport, one of its most transitional spaces, a conduit through which people are constantly in motion. Her look is not direct or documentary, but is figured through an array of photographic feints and circumstantial filters. The silver airplanes, when they appear in the field of these photo-maneuvers, are images of technological potential flashing into view, myths of motion with

23

LAX Dai Ichi
2002

24 LAX Sea Breeze Inn
2002

bright steel skin. Seen through the window, their appearance evinces the most powerful dreams of modern travel: passive immersion in the endless flow of travel, anonymity, luxury, freedom from the passing of time, freedom – here we might recall Baudelaire's splenetic poem *"N'importe où hors du monde"* – from the burden of being a person at all.

This is a dream from which Crosher always seems to be waking up. A mirage, shimmering, bent in the sun. It flickers into sight then recedes, disappears. The plane is grounded, and the trip is over. The traveler off-boards, and enters into the bustling corporate zocalo. She pays a stoned employee three dollars pulled from her bag, and sips a reconstituted orange juice from a clear plastic cup. She checks if the mobile's got bars, pulls down her jacket, and marks time until her bags emerge. Piss. Pass some time. Home again.

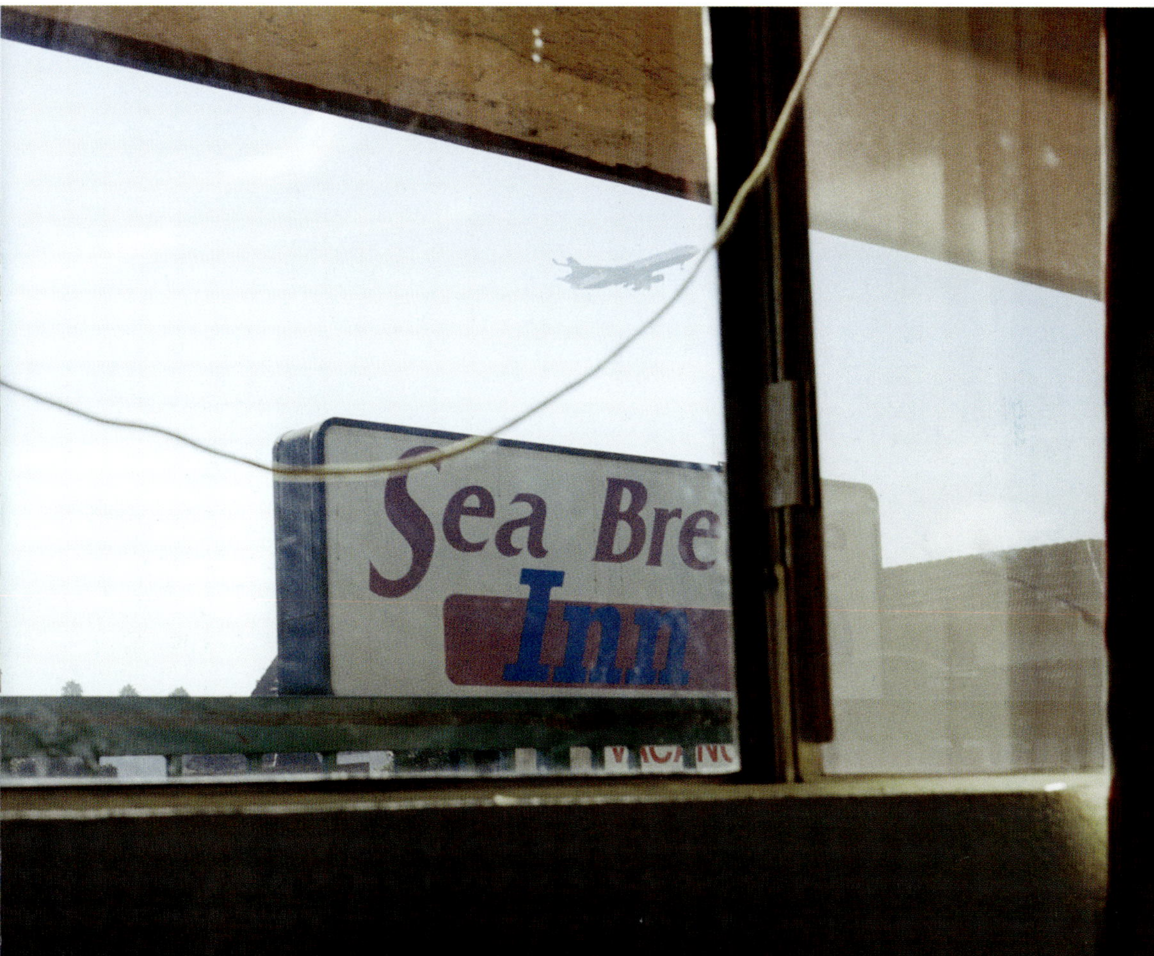
Sea Bre
Inn

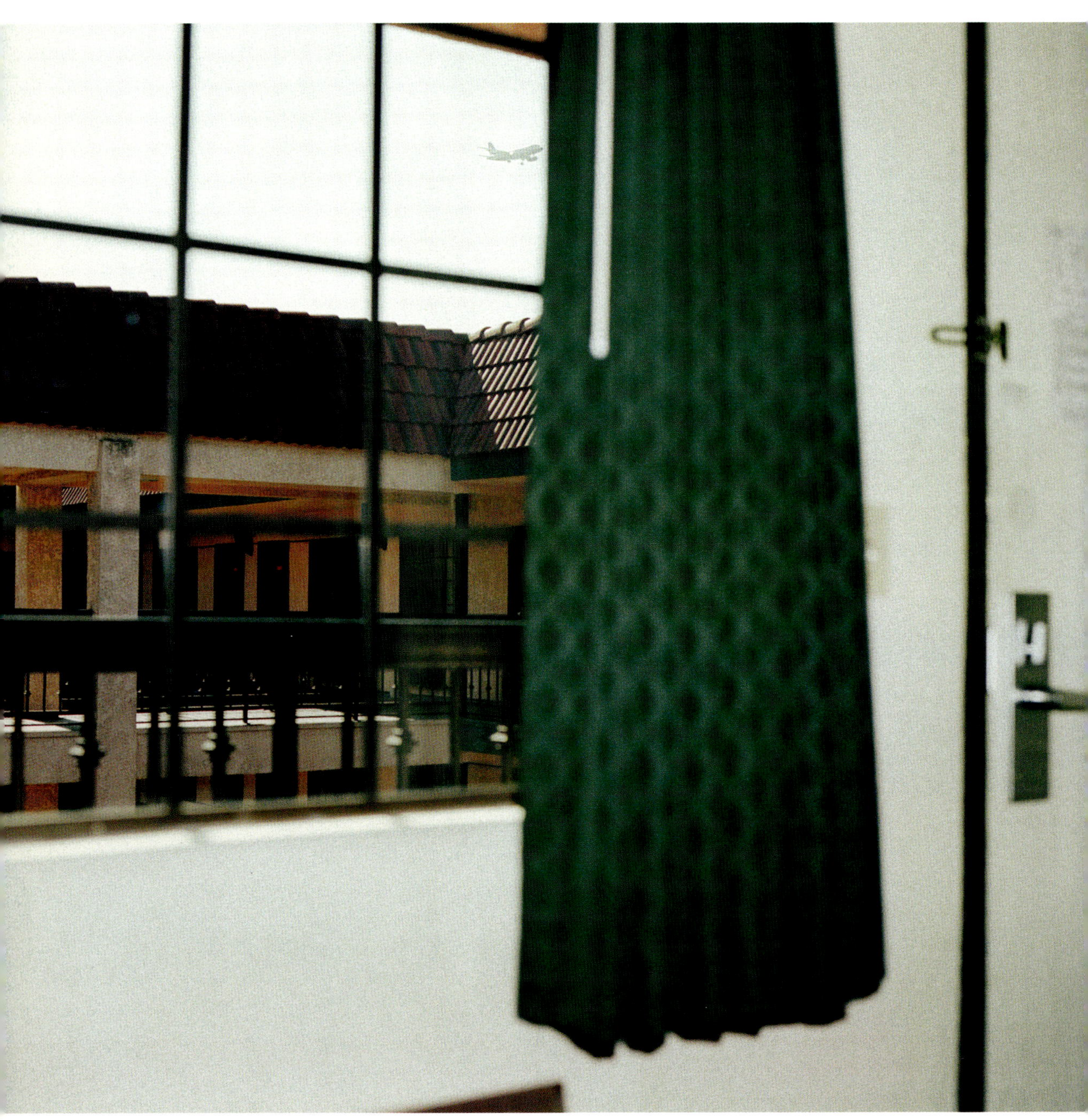

Crosher's photographs picture time passing slowly in a world where everything is supposed to be traveling quickly. This airport is missing all the people conceivably moving about, inhabiting planes and leaving them, driving, sleeping, eating, fucking in the rooms, or arguing in the carport. None of that finds a place in the pictures; there is no city-bustle, just solitude. The room is empty and still; bags of fast food, indices of habitation, are scattered across the table; chips of paint flake from the grille of the radiator. The hotel fills the photograph, overwhelms the punctum of the aircraft with details seen in the muted half-light of the hotel suite. Time passes but slowly; the claustrophobic ecstasy of travel dissipates into a narcotic haze. [...]

He must have stared at the map for hours, these red vectors drawn over the mottled topography

25

LAX Ramada
2003

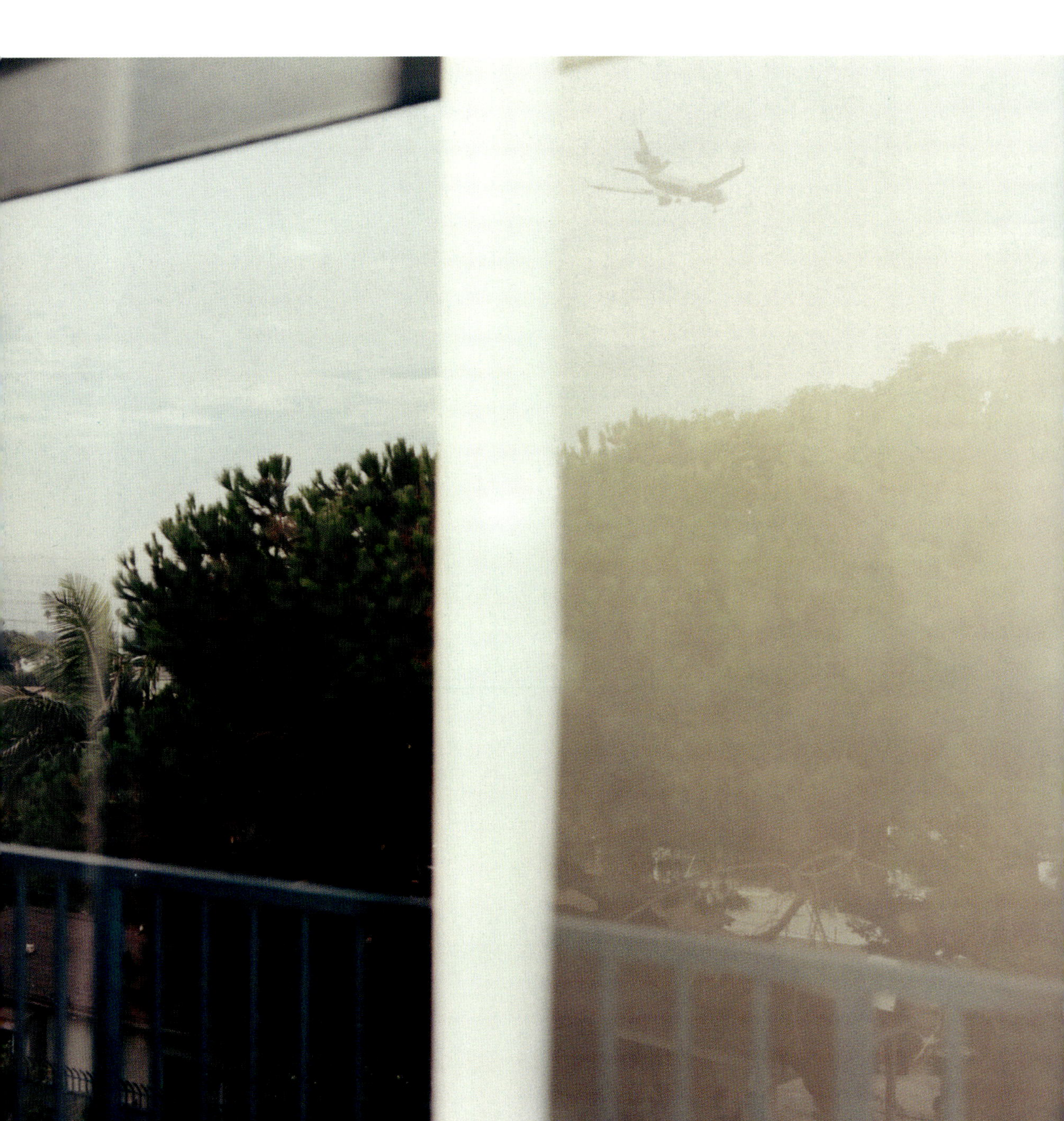

of North America. "Travel Instantly From City To City," implied the hot red lines: "You'll Get There in No Time!" *But I'm just sitting here waiting,* he thought. *I'm in the air and it's boring. Fuck's sake, I've got all the time in the world!* He reached under the seat for his camera.

26

LAX Super 8
2003

During a transcontinental flight from New York City to Los Angeles, artist Douglas Huebler (1924-1997) took a snapshot out the window over each state as he flew over it, mapping an abstract system of borders from the air. The final version of the project called *Location Piece #1, New York-Los Angeles, February 1969* collected the map, several photographs in no particular order, and a typescript:

In February, 1969, the airspace over each of the thirteen states between New York and Los

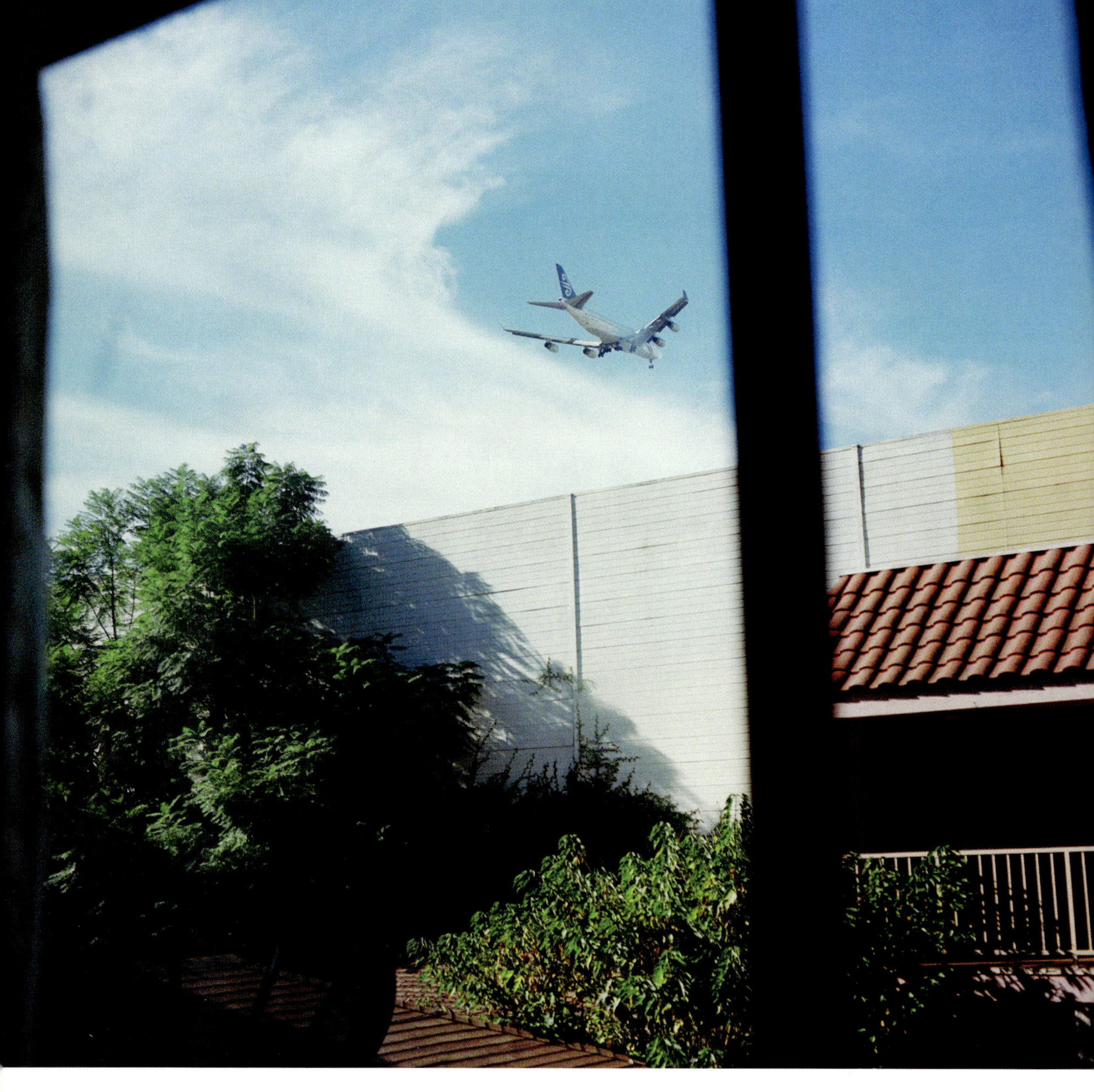

Angeles was documented by a photograph made as the camera was pointed more or less straight out the airplane window (with no "interesting" view intended). The photographs join together the East and West coasts of the United States as each serves to "mark" one of the thirteen states flown over during that particular flight.[3]

The square silver photographs were not organized or "keyed" to their particular states; each photograph looks dreamily the same. His collected data is mediated to the point of oblivion, registering only blurs of clouds and sky through the glass of the airplane window. The rigor of his conceptual project purports to quasi-scientifically record the direct experience of his situation with little fanfare or expressive intent, but instead reveals a delirious field of clouds and sky. In these images, the very "logic" of collected

27 LAX Royal Comfort Motel
2005

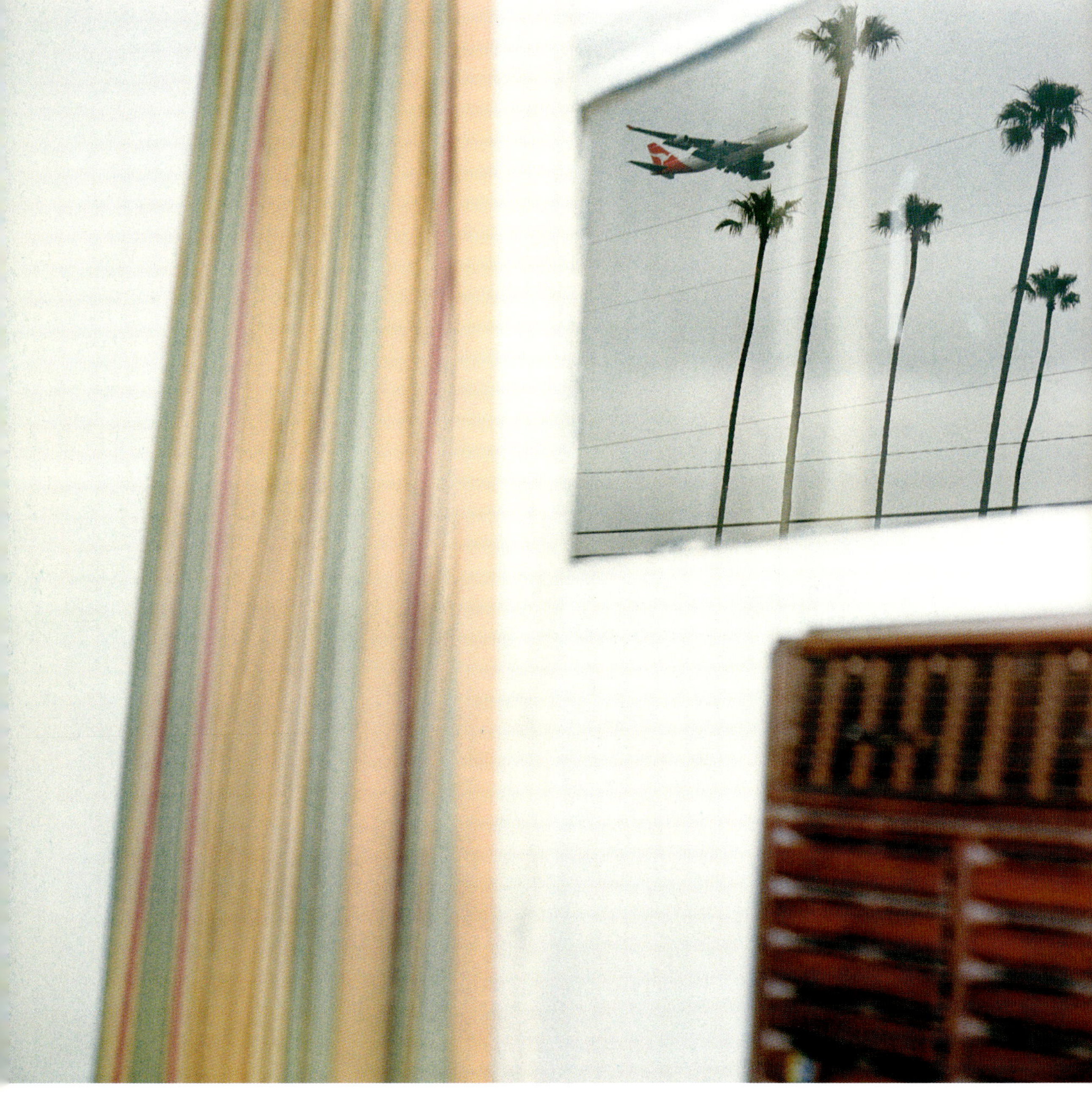

information is eroded by the contingency of its point of view – the very thing that might have shored up its "specificity". Simple structures produce unexpected outcomes. The sky over Pennsylvania is indistinguishable from that above Nevada. "Conceptual artists are mystics rather than rationalists," began Sol LeWitt, composing his "Sentences on Conceptual Art" in 1969; "I wish Conceptual art was dead," replied one of the respondents in Huebler's survey at the Jewish Museum in 1970, which asked its participants to exchange confidential secrets. ("I have recently wanted to go all the way with a boy," said another; "I am a truly fucked up person," confided a third.)[4]

Crosher's best photographs give her conceptual program a delirious visuality foreign to conceptual photography circa 1970, and it is this that separates her from other people who've taken

28

LAX Adventurer Hotel
2003

29 LAX Econolodge
2003

pictures of LA before her – Ed Ruscha and Catherine Opie being only two examples. I am thinking of the indistinct pinky-blue coverlet simmering up to meet a warped radiator in 'LAX Caesar's Motel', and the smeared sunstroke that washes over the shabby strip mall in 'LAX Best Western Suites'. Among the more prosaic photographs these have the flair of poetry, giving the series a sudden emotionality that's unexpected and affecting. Their sun-warped eroticism reminds me of My Bloody Valentine's 'To Here Knows When' or 'Cigarette in Your Bed'. People fuck in hotels, too.

I first came across Crosher's work in the late 1990s, pictures of people I knew, flamboyant thrift-punks dressed up and gorgeous. It was work about self-presentation and self-consciousness, and learning about people by

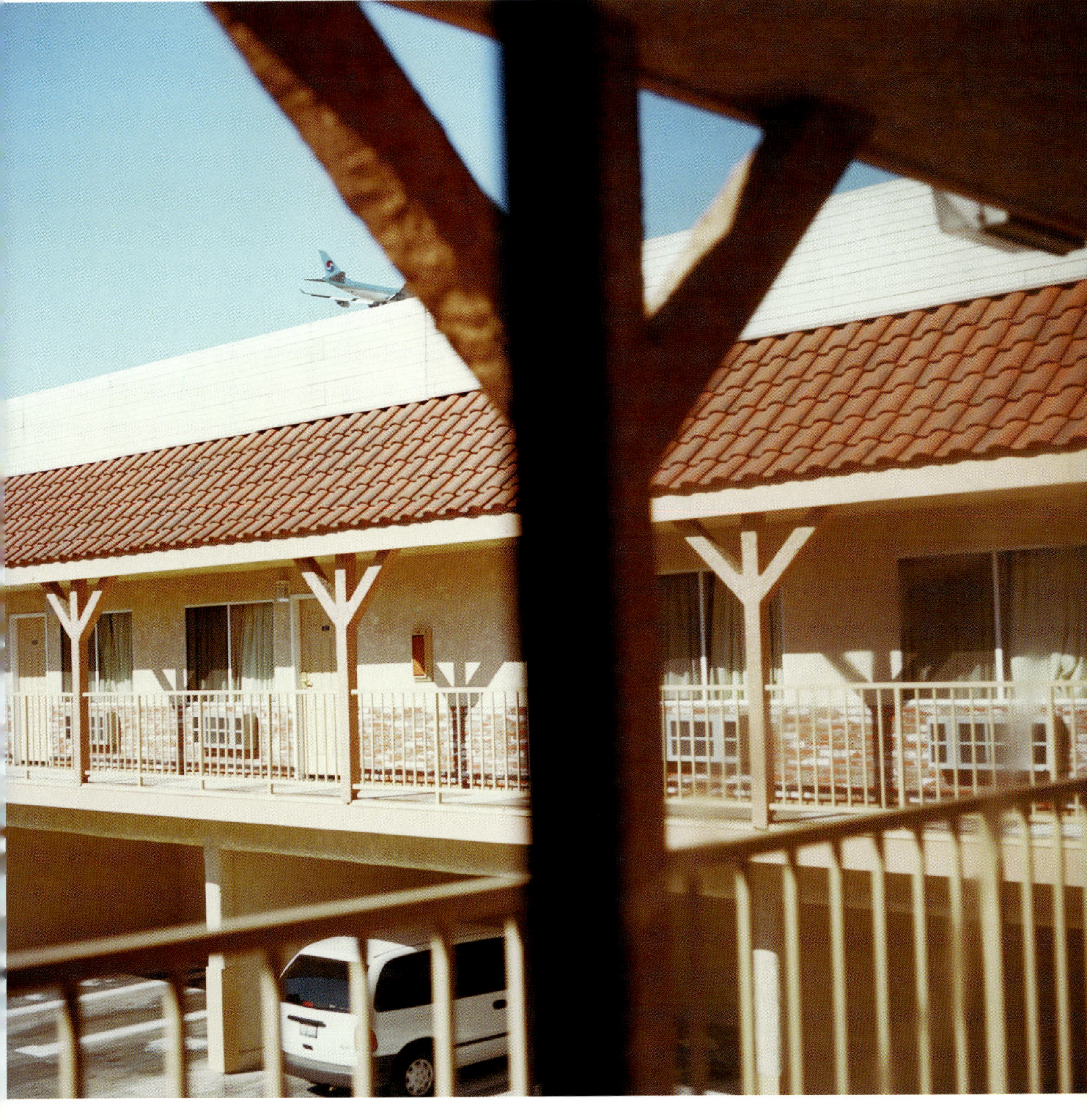

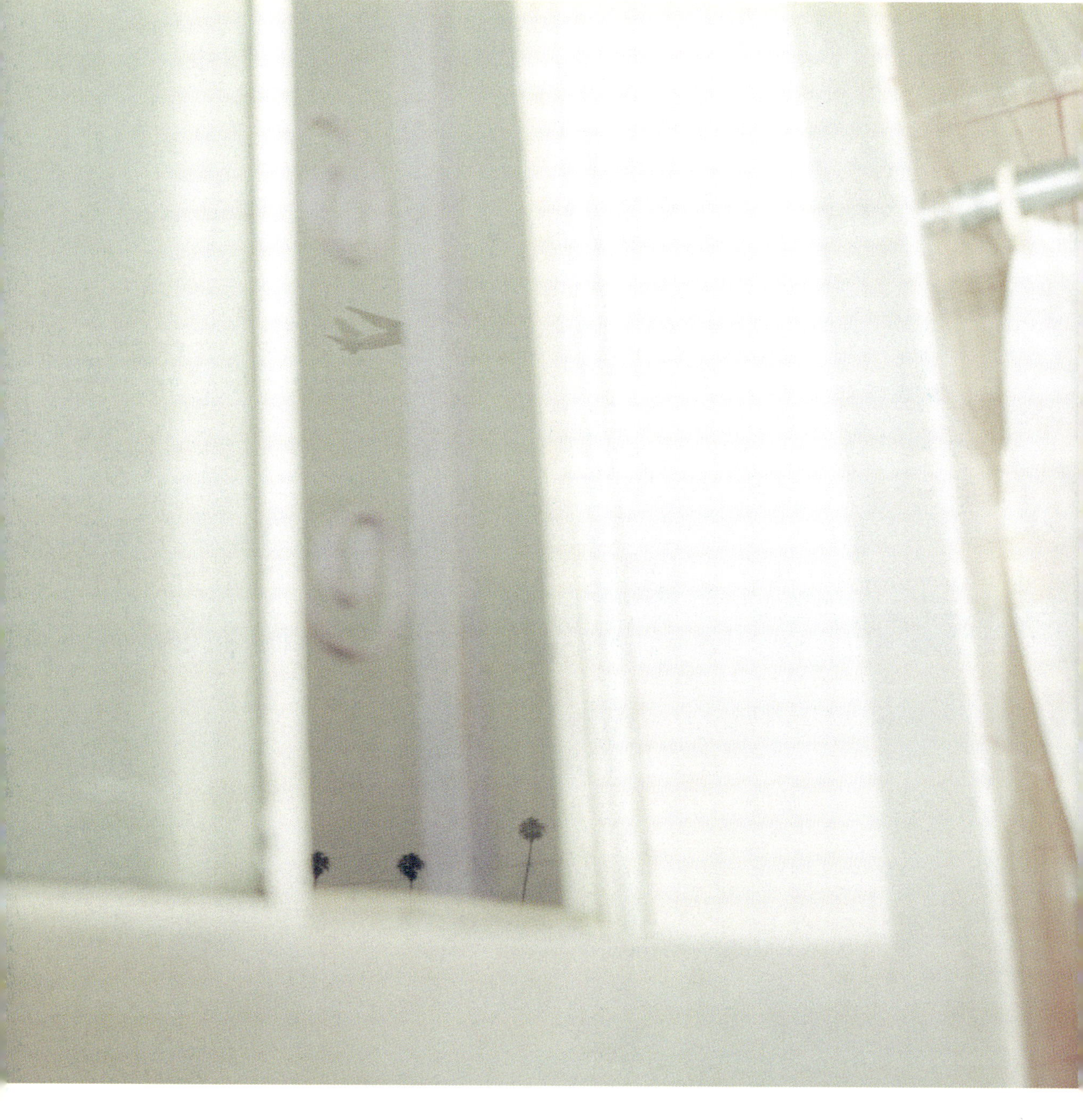

taking pictures of them. They are pictures jammed with anthropological detail, queer bangs and polyester shirts, odd posters in aging kitchens. So let's say that her new series is quite sublimated in comparison. But, as T.S. Eliot wrote in 1920,

Poetry is not a turning loose of emotion, but an escape from emotion; it is not the expression of personality, but an escape from personality. But, of course, only those who have personality and emotions know what it means to want to escape from these things.[5]

30 LAX Airport Hotel
2005

[1] LeWitt, Sol. 1967. "Paragraphs on Conceptual Art." In *Artforum* (June, 1967).

[2] Crosher, Zoe. Unpublished artist's statement, 2004.

[3] Lippard, Lucy. *Six Years: The Dematerialization of the Art Object from 1966-1972...* Berkeley and Los Angeles:

31 LAX Hollycrest
2005

University of California Press, 1997.

[4] Cited by James Meyer in "Global Conceptualism: Points of Origin 1950s-1980s (review)." *Artforum* (September 1999); originally printed in Douglas Huebler, *Variable Piece 4: Secrets*. New York: Printed Matter, 1973.

[5] Eliot, T. S. "Tradition and the Individual Talent." *In The Sacred Wood; essays on poetry and criticism.* London: Methuen, 1920.

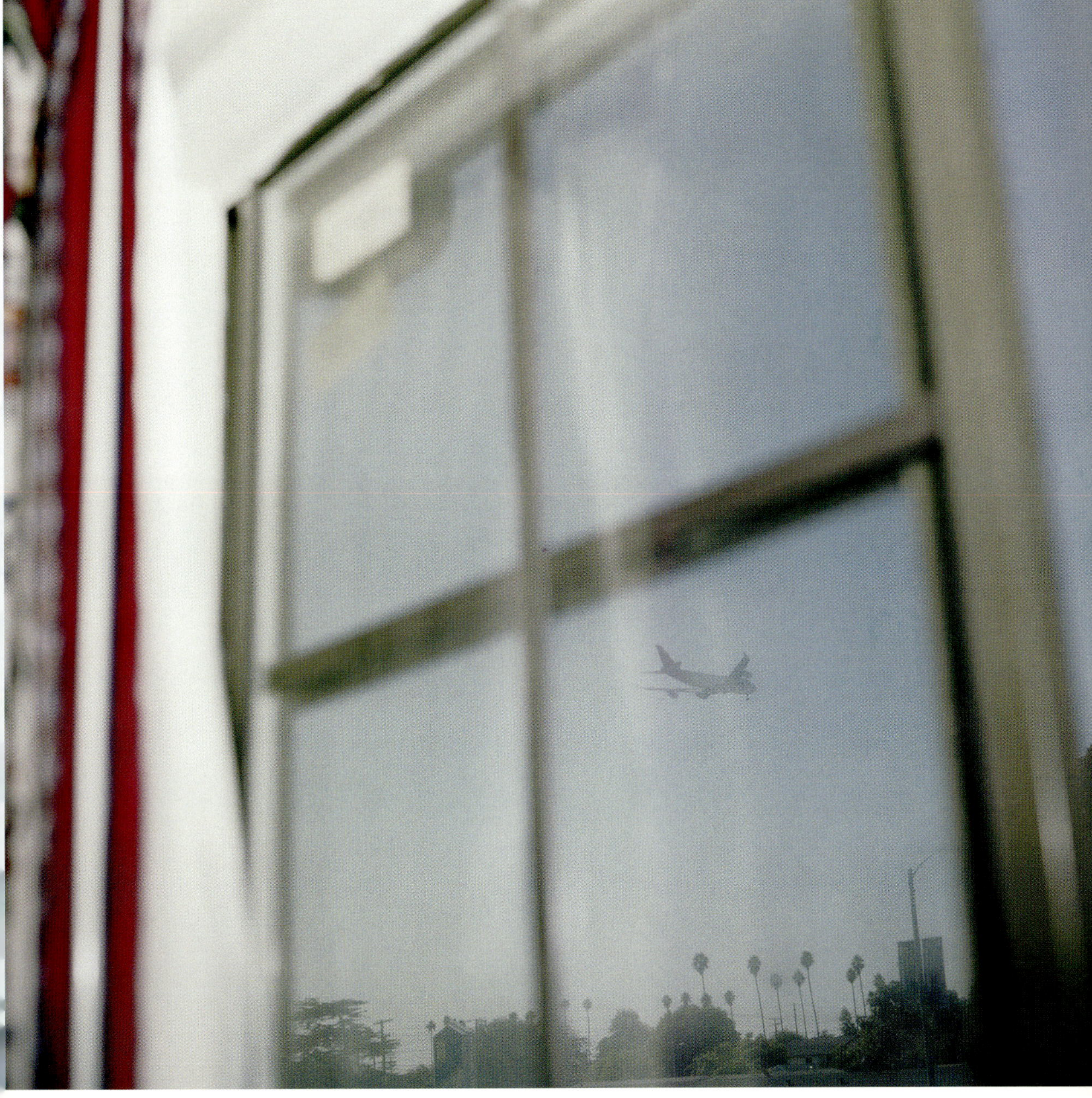

BIOGRAPHIES

PICO IYER is the author of several books about cultures crossing, including *Video Night in Kathmandu*, *The Lady and the Monk*, *The Global Soul* and *Abandon*. He lives in Japan when not on his way to North Korea, Easter Island or Ethiopia.

Cultural critic and novelist, NORMAN KLEIN is the author of *The History of Forgetting: Los Angeles and the Erasure of Memory*, *The Vatican to Vegas: The History of Special Effects*, *Seven Minutes: Life and Death of the American Animated Cartoon*, *Bleeding Through: Layers of Los Angeles* (DVD-ROM), *Freud in Coney Island*, and in 2007, *The Imaginary Twentieth Century* (DVD-ROM). He is a professor at the California Institute of the Arts.

JULIAN MYERS is a critic, historian, and curator whose writings have appeared in *Documents*, *October*, *Afterall* , *frieze*, and other periodicals. His published works include essays *Ellsworth Kelly in San Francisco* (2002), *Sightlines* (2005), and *Super-Pride and Super Prejudice* (2005). He is an assistant professor at the California College of the Arts.

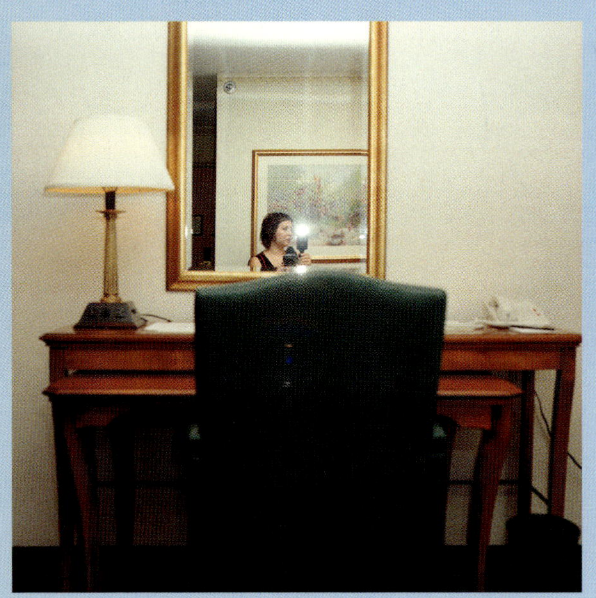

Me at the LAX Marriott
2003

As Julian Myers writes, "ZOE CROSHER'S method works through the difficulty of taking pictures of Los Angeles, and what she understands as its resistance to being pictured." This obsession with capturing the imaginary of LA began with the series *Out The Window (LAX)* (2001-05). By photographing planes coming in to land from each motel along the forgotten strip of Century Boulevard by LAX, Zoe Crosher captures the dreams deferred and absorbed into the anonymity of these transient spaces. Her interest in what she calls, "a place that moves in shifts and perpetual motion, with no real center, no point of concentration," now informs the series *LA-Like* (2004-present), a body of work inspired by the sun-drenched noir of Raymond Chandler and the anodyne boosterism of Helen Hunt Jackson and the other early salesmen of the Los Angeles proto-myth. By both blackening the prints and negatives in post-production and other times shooting directly into the sun, Crosher, in *LA-Like*, merges the poetics of burning with the medium itself.

Other projects include *The Reconsidered Archive of Michelle du Bois*, clusters of tourist, performative, and posed images of and by duBois shot in post-WWII Pacific Rim cities during the 70s and 80s and reconfigured by Crosher. Also the transformative series *1 Yr Later*, diptychs of girls from all over the US photographed in identical scenarios in their last year of high school and again exactly a year later.

Playing with fictional documentary, the fantasy of expectation and the false promise of travel, an obsession with transience, and the reconsidered archive, her work has been shown internationally in Vancouver, Rotterdam, Los Angeles, and New York City. She completed her MFA at the California Institute of the Arts in the Photography and Integrated Media Programs in 2001. After editing *NTNTNT* (2004), a collaborative project investigating the short-lived history of net. art, she continues work as the U.S. Project Manager for *Afterall A Journal of Art Context & Inquiry*. The daughter of a diplomat and airline stewardess, she is for the moment settled in Los Angeles.

Thank you

Andrew Berardini, Magda Berliner, Deric Carner, DCKT Contemporary, Fred Daniel, Lauri Firstenberg, Laurel Gitlen, Paul Graves, Eleanor Harwood, Pico Iyer, Norman Klein, LA Cultural Affairs Office, Alex MacBride, Tom Marble (LA Forum), Lee Michel, Julian Myers, Steffie Nelson, Michael Pinto (LA Forum), Megan Riley, Simon Storey, Sino Wong, Mark Wyse & Ted Young-Ing. Special thanks to Allan Sekula & Norman Klein for planting the seed; the Westin Los Angeles Airport, Los Angeles Airport Marriot & The Crowne Plaza Hotel Los Angeles-Intl Airport for complimentary use of their rooms; and finally to all the people that kept me company during the shoots...

This project would not be possible without the generous support of Philip E. Aarons and Shelley Fox Aarons; The Crosher Family; and The Penny McCall Foundation, New York.